THE CHILD AND REALITY

The Child and Reality

Lectures by a Child Psychiatrist

T. A. RATCLIFFE MA, MB, DPM, DCH

London
GEORGE ALLEN & UNWIN LTD
RUSKIN HOUSE · MUSEUM STREET

FIRST PUBLISHED IN 1970

ISBN 0 04 616010 8

PRINTED IN GREAT BRITAIN
in 11pt Plantin
UNWIN BROTHERS LTD
WOKING AND LONDON

Author's Introduction

Although many present-day experts in the art of 'communication' and teaching have tended to condemn the lecturer-audience situation as outmoded by comparison with group discussion techniques, the lecture appears to be holding its own quite adequately. Indeed, it seems likely that, with the modern trend towards more and more conferences and the like, even more lectures are being given nowadays.

As someone who has been invited to give (and, indeed, has given) a very large number of lectures to audiences of varying degrees of professional expertise and active concern with the chosen topic, the present writer inevitably has given considerable attention and thought to the role of the lecturer; and to the functions and techniques of lecturing, as opposed to group discussion. Some of these views have been included in a booklet published by the National Marriage Guidance Council (*The Functioning of Groups*, T. A. Ratcliffe, NMGC Training Monographs). Some additional brief comments on the value and limitations of lecture techniques would seem to be appropriate here however.

A lecture, which is later published as a technical paper, is probably the ideal method of giving factual, and already proven, information. But a lecture can have a much wider function also, as this book hopes to demonstrate.

In a personal communication made to the present writer some years ago, a distinguished colleague with a vast experience in the art of communication (the late Dr J. R. Rees) gave the following as his ideal basis for this wider concept of lecturing:

> 'Such a lecture must be stimulating and interesting. It should provide, as coherently as possible and in a way which is acceptable to, and understandable by, the particular audience at which it is aimed, the carefully thought-out ideas of the lecturer. Yet such ideas must not be stated as the final and absolute decision of the 'expert'. Their purpose should be to stimulate the audience's own thinking on the topic.'

Although I would never claim to have achieved the very high standards in this field of 'J.R.' himself, this is the model which I, too, have tried to follow when lecturing.

A lecture, however, is an ephemeral event, particularly when one uses neither written notes nor prepared script. Its impact is limited to the size of the audience, be this fifty or five hundred; and even when it is tape-recorded and reproduced in the journal of the organization to which the lecture was originally given, its impact will be largely restricted still to the same 'interest group'.

When, therefore, I found myself being invited quite often to repeat a particular lecture on a later occasion, and to a different type of audience (as was the case with the majority of the lectures in this book), I felt that such lectures might have an appeal, and value, to a wider and multi-disciplinary audience. Hence the suggestion for their publication as a book. To justify such action, however, it was clearly essential to convert the spoken word into a more 'literary' style; and to rearrange the content for such a wider audience. Although, therefore, the lectures in this book are based on the form in which they were originally given, some additions and amendments have been made to include, for example, points which arose in the various discussions which followed many of these lectures.

Critics of books of this type (including the present writer in his capacity of reviewer!) have complained of the inevitable repetition of various topics from lecture to lecture. This criticism is certainly true of this particular book; but since such repetitions represent some of my basic professional 'philosophy', I have let these remain. Equally, in choosing which actual lectures were to be included in this volume, my main aim has been to select topics which bear some relationship with each other. My hope, therefore, is that such repetitions as are inevitable will enable the book to be considered and read as a coherent whole, rather than as a series of separate lectures.

The final chapter of this book is an exception to this rule, however. It is, moreover, 'dated' in that this particular lecture was delivered at a National Association for Mental Health Annual Conference in 1949. It is included here to illustrate how far a prediction of future Community Mental Health trends has been justified by the developments of such services in the past twenty years.

In a book of this type, where each chapter is a separate lecture, each on a different subject, it is impossible to find any title which would cover adequately, or give a composite description of, the book as a whole. Some comment, therefore, seems necessary to justify and explain the actual title which I have chosen for this book.

I would be amongst the last to deny the significance and importance of an adequate study and understanding of unconscious factors when working with children—or adults. A great deal has been written on these aspects; but very much less comment is available on the need to balance the impact and significance of the reality situation against such unconscious motivations. Since the necessary achievement of such a balance is one recurring theme in many of the chapters of this book, and since I regard it as a very important theme, it seemed justified to stress this aspect in the title of the book itself.

T.A.R.

Acknowledgements

Most of the lectures included in this book have been given on quite a number of occasions in differing forms and to different types of audience. It would be both tedious and unnecessary to list all these varying occasions here.

A number of the lectures, however, were given, at least initially, on some specific occasion, the lecture being subsequently printed in the journal or report of the particular organization which sponsored the actual 'special occasion'. In these instances, I am greatly indebted to the organizations concerned for their consent to include the lectures in this book.

Specifically, I would like to express my acknowledgements and gratitude over the following items in the book.

Chapter I: This lecture was originally delivered at the 1969 Annual Conference of the Association of Workers with Maladjusted Children: I am grateful for their agreement to the publication of this lecture both in this book and in the report of that Conference.
Chapter VII: This contribution was the concluding, and summing-up, paper at the 1968 Annual Conference of the National Association of Maternal and Child Welfare; it was subsequently included in the report of that Conference. I am indebted to Miss D. Hall, General Secretary of the Association for agreement to include this lecture here.
Chapters VIII and XII: These lectures were originally delivered at National Association of Mental Health Annual Conferences; both were included in the report of those two Conferences. I am grateful to Miss M. Appleby, MA, JP, General Secretary of NAMH for consent to reproduce this material in this book. I should stress that for Chapter VIII, although I have leaned heavily on the original lecture given at that Inter-Clinic Conference, I have amended it considerably here to the form in which it has been given subsequently to different, and more 'general' audiences.
Chapter IX: This lecture was first delivered to a London Meeting of the Association of Psychiatric Social Workers: and subsequently published in the *British Journal of Psychiatric Social Work.* I acknowledge with thanks the agreement of the Editor of the Journal to include the lecture in this book.
Chapter X: Although given on other occasions also, this was an Institute for the Scientific Study of Delinquency Public Lecture in London; it was subsequently included as one section of an ISTD Pamphlet, 'The Problem Family' (ISTD, 8 Bourdon Street, Davies Street, London, W.1: 1958). I am very grateful to Miss Eve Saville,

MBE, General Secretary of the ISTD for consent to use this lecture material here.
Chapter XI: Although this lecture has been given in various forms at a number of Colleges of Education, it was originally delivered at a Tri-partite Conference organized in 1967 at Loughborough University by the Society of Medical Officers of Health, the Association of Teachers in Colleges and Departments of Education and the Central Council for Health Education. It was reproduced in shorter form in the Conference Report, and in *Health Education.* In its present form it appeared in *Public Health.* I am grateful to Dr J. D. Kershaw, Chairman of the Editorial Board of that Journal, for consent to use the material in this book.

T.A.R.

Contents

Chapter I

Residential Work with Children
Treatment or Training—Is there a Difference?

It is a remarkable but relevant fact that it should be considered necessary by those with many years' experience in residential work with 'maladjusted' children to discuss these two alternative forms of help for such children as if there were always these two completely different alternatives between which one must choose in each case. Even more significant is the subtle implication in our thinking that 'training' is always of inferior status in comparison with 'treatment'. Yet there are understandable reasons for basic attitudes such as these.

All professional workers tend to over-use, and misuse, 'jargon'; and, in particular, to give special technical meanings to words which have another significance when used in ordinary conversation. Consequently, there is often considerable confusion as to what each of us means by 'treatment' or 'training'.

Secondly, there is a very wide range of differing types of residential unit. In part such differences stem from the varying roles and personalities of those in charge of individual units; but, more importantly, each individual unit has tended to 'specialize' in a different type of problem, and thus choose the type of child whom that particular unit can help most effectively. This high degree of specialization is one of the most valuable, and necessary, features of residential work in this country; but it also means that each of us will tend to regard his own personal techniques of training or treatment not only as the most genuinely suitable for the children in *his* unit, but also as the ideal for all other units equally.

The problem can be vividly illustrated by considering the

question of treatment in its narrowest, psychotherapeutic sense. It has been estimated that, in the average local education authority hostel, less than ½ per cent of the children in that type of setting will require long-term intensive psychotherapy (with an additional 5 per cent who may need skilled professional counselling help from time to time). In a hospital children's or adolescent unit, their higher proportion of deeply disturbed patients will mean that psychotherapy is much more widely needed and used. Finally, in those one or two schools which specialize in, and therefore select, only children with deep neurotic disturbance, the proportion of children requiring intensive psychotherapeutic treatment may rise virtually to 100 per cent.

Few workers in this field, and certainly not I myself, would deny the necessity for such forms of treatment when these are needed. Nevertheless, it is equally essential to remember that, for the majority of children in this type of special school, hostel or unit, the 'treatment' of choice is not psychotherapy but that form of help which has been described as 'relationship therapy' or 'environmental therapy'. That is to say, the deliberate development and provision of a régime and setting within which, and because of which, the child can mature and adjust both happily and successfully; and within which he (or she) can build up satisfactory relationships both with adults and with his own peers. There are indeed two important basic reasons which justify this types of help as the treatment of choice, in the great majority of such cases.

Children, and even more so, adolescents, tend to act out their problems and difficulties in real life situations rather than to verbalize such difficulties in the way which many adults do. It would be wrong to deny the significance of unconscious factors when working with children; but it must be remembered that youth is much nearer to a normal use and understanding of fantasy than is the adult; and the child's defences are much less sophisticated and elaborate than these will be in adulthood. Consequently, when one is working with children, it seems reasonable to attribute relatively much greater importance and significance to reality factors than to unconscious ones.

Another important factor is that the only really positive criterion to justify any sort of residential placement for a child is that the placement chosen can provide something which the child needs, but which cannot be provided, even with help, within the child's own family home. An obvious example of this principle is that one would not (or, at least, one should not!), admit a child to a paediatric hospital unless he requires some form of nursing, treatment or investigation which would not be possible in his own home. This same basic principle applies equally to any form of residential placement for children. What otherwise 'unobtainable' form of help do we therefore try to offer to the maladjusted child when we advise on residential placement for him or her?

The short and simple answer to this question would be that we try to provide a good adult contact; or, in rather more sophisticated terms, we aim to provide an additional (or substitute) parental image and relationship. Yet these apparently simple provisions require careful analysis before they can have any real meaning or purpose. Perhaps, therefore, it would be more accurate to say that the aim should be to provide those parts of the parental image, and those parts of the child's past environmental experience which have been defective or missing.

For the severely deprived child, this may involve the provision of a permanent and total substitute mother-and-father relationship. But for some children and especially for those whom we aim to return to their own families in due course, the need may well be to provide temporarily a more suitable father-figure *or* mother-figure; and here one must always clearly bear in mind the very differing roles of a mother or a father *vis-à-vis* infant, or child or adolescent. More often still, it may be one *part* of the parental image that is defective. Has this adolescent lacked the necessary authority aspects of the father's role; or this small child the equally necessary protective role of the mother? Has this teenage girl had no adult male figure with whom she can safely and securely 'flirt' and try out her developing femininity? If so, must not the residential unit provide just these requirements?

Similarly, on the general environmental side, the child or adolescent may have lacked adequate 'cultural' stimulus; he may have been pushed too hard and have had too much demanded of him socially or educationally. He may have grown up in a family which itself had no stable standards, and could set no suitable example for him. Or, perhaps most commonly of all, he or she may have had a lifelong and successful experience of manipulating every situation to his own demands in the face of weak, ineffectual, unsure or inconsistent parental handling.

Clearly very different types of relationship and environmental therapy must be provided in each of these differing circumstances. Yet, even so, each form of treatment or training has one central and essential factor in common. The relationship must be with a 'real adult' reacting in 'real life' situations. What has been vividly described as 'synthetic geniality' will cut no ice at all. Nor will the parental role be of any value if the adult himself behaves immaturely. The teenager who urgently needs (and demands, if most often indirectly) a stable, adult figure upon whom to rely will not be helped if that adult attempts to be a pseudo-adolescent himself in order to curry favour or gain popularity. Nor will the substitute (or real) parent succeed if he sidesteps reality situations and difficulties, instead of helping the child, or even more so, the adolescent, to cope with such problems.

'Real' people, however, can be cross as well as pleased; can say 'no' as well as 'yes'; and can be disapproving as well as approving as each is necessary or appropriate. Inevitably, therefore, questions of discipline must play an important part in the work of any residential unit.

It is unfortunate that the word 'discipline' (like 'training') is so often used in a derogatory and condemnatory way. Although discipline is so often, but mistakenly, seen in terms of punishment, restriction and rules, it is, in fact, the achievement of a good and mature balance between necessary freedom and equally necessary control. Obviously it will require the development of an adequate degree of self-discipline based on the individual's own internalized standards and powers of self-control and self-decision to achieve such a balance in its most complete form. But it is difficult to see how these individual controls and standards can be internalized except on the initial basis of adequate externally imposed standards, encouragement, controls and example within the framework of the child's experience and relationships. One has only to observe the normal maturation and emotional and social growth of any child to recognize the gradual transition from external to internalized discipline. It seems remarkable, therefore, to suggest that we should deny this same basic requirement to disturbed children in a residential setting, especially since, for a variety of reasons and in different ways, the great majority of such children will have lacked—in part or in full—this essential part of life experience. If a residential unit staff member does not provide this requirement adequately, consistently and firmly, *is* he providing what the child has so far lacked; or, for that matter, is he being that necessary figure for the child—a 'real adult'?

Few of those with adequate experience with children, would claim that one could successfully 'bring up' or help any child solely on the basis of punishments or rewards; but this is not the same thing as saying that such factors and methods do not have a part in the necessary total environmental and relationship needs of the child.

This does not mean, of course, that one must work only within an elaborate frame of rules, or so supervise and control the child that he has no opportunity for experiment or growth. What it does mean is that one balances approval and disapproval against each other as each is 'earned'; that one knows when to encourage and when to prohibit; when to take action and when to leave alone; and, above all, to know what demands can and should be made on the child in terms of his maturity, his capacity and his needs at that moment of time. Any setting which is to achieve this must be reasonably structured; but the essential aim is to provide, maintain and indicate clearly the boundaries of acceptable behaviour (in the widest sense of that word), thus creating a known framework within which the child can experiment securely and learn how to cope successfully, and without excessive anxiety, with problems and stresses which are within his capacity at that stage.

It is also important to recognize that, in a residential setting, one does not establish and maintain these boundaries, or build up the necessary child–adult relationship, solely by dealing successfully with a major behaviour crisis—although sometimes this can be a valuable and necessary starting point. Far more frequently, however, it is the way in which the adult handles, and reacts to, the everyday incidents of the living-together situation, and the total régime and 'atmosphere' which he creates which are the really significant factors in achieving such success.

It will be obvious that much of what has been described above could be classified as 'training'. Yet can there be any doubt that it is also treatment and therapy involving a very high order of technical skill?

Where does the child psychiatrist (who for so long has seen the therapy of the disturbed child as his own private province) stand in all this? Certainly he will have to come out from his ivory tower, and learn to recognize, and to respect, the treatment skills and roles of workers in residential units. He must willingly accept that his own treatment function *vis-à-vis* the individual child in such a setting will be a small and limited one. But this is not to say that he does not, or should not, have another equally important task.

Like every other specialist, the child psychiatrist has two separate, but closely interrelated, professional functions. First he must assess and select such children as need his particular treatment skills; and provide that therapy for them. But his second, and consultative role, is the more important in the situations with which we are here concerned.

If the residential worker is to carry out his complex treatment task as we have described it here, he (or she) must be a stable adult who has worked out his own attitudes (and prejudices) maturely and with insight. This raises the issue of good selection of such workers—and one could spend a whole conference on that topic alone! Equally one could, and indeed should, give detailed thought to the structure and type of staff training courses which would best increase both the technical skills of residential staffs, and their insight into human motivation and behaviour. Yet even if we ever achieved this standard of good selection and well-balanced training, the consultant would still have a vital and necessary role.

Residential work with children is a very demanding task in which one is 'giving' a great deal; and however well-integrated the unit is within the local community, it is also a very isolating task. For this reason alone the understanding visitor 'from outside' has a valuable function for staff morale. But the consultant's real role goes more deeply than this.

Whilst it would be generally agreed that the residential worker must avoid a too intense or too deep emotional entanglement with the child whom he hopes to help, *some* degree of emotional feeling and involvement may well be a vital factor if such help is to be really effective. Moreover, however carefully the worker preserves his own professional attitude, he will still have to be aware of, and cope with, the child's natural feelings for him whether these be negative or positive.

In practice, this delicate balance between too much and too little involvement is almost impossible to achieve in a residential setting without the help of a skilled and understanding 'outsider'. There will be other and equal complex decisions to be made; when to intervene and when to leave well alone; when to prohibit and when to encourage; when to be protective and when to push; and many others. Moreover, each of these decisions has to be made in terms of the individual child's needs at that particular moment of time; and within the emotionally changing dynamic pattern of the residential community.

Although it is, and indeed most often should be, the worker who has to handle these actual day-to-day situations, the child psychiatrist, with his specialized knowledge of human behaviour and motivation, and his relatively more 'detached' view of the total situation can provide insight, confidence and support to the worker in his task. He can provide the 'diagnosis' upon which the most appropriate 'treatment' can be based.

It would be inappropriate to discuss in detail here the child psychiatrist's total consultant role or his own relationship with the children; but certain essential features must be noted.

Quite often, indeed probably most often, the psychiatrist's contribution may appear to be a 'negative' one in that he is stressing that this is not a psychiatrically sick child. Yet, if the worker can be helped to accept this reassurance, he can apply with confidence his techniques of handling the 'normal' child. Equally importantly, the psychiatrist, in explaining the child's behaviour and its motivation, is not excusing that behaviour. In other words, he is stressing that normal guilt and normal anxiety are constructive mechanisms which are necessary for satisfactory character and personality growth.

Nor is it the child psychiatrist's role to tell the residential worker *how* he should handle the situation, or the child, but to help the worker to use his own skills, insight and ability more confidently and successfully.

If we are to achieve real co-operation—and without such co-operation the whole enterprise will fail—there must be mutual trust in, and respect for, each other's skills and personalities; and an ability to accept genuinely not only each other's limitations and strengths, but our own limitations and strengths also.

Chapter II

The Therapeutic Team in a Residential Hostel Setting

All professions build up a technical language of their own which is then valuably used as a means of communication within the specialist group; but the boundary between a constructive use of technical jargon, and its misuse, is a narrow one. It is, therefore, dangerously easy to overstep this boundary without our recognizing that we have done so. We can become so accustomed to using our jargon phrases that these end as a series of clichés about whose original meaning we have long since ceased to think. In my own speciality, for example, the phrase 'the deprived child' had a specific, important and limited significance when it was first brought into use. Now it is often used loosely to mean any child who is deprived of almost anything that the speaker thinks he ought to have. There is an even more dangerous risk, however, when our jargon is given a 'mystique' of its own: or if we give it our unthinking acceptance, and do not analyse just why we are doing so. That now popular jargon term, 'the team approach', has suffered this fate to become one of the 'sacred cows' of quite a number of professions. But what exactly does this term mean, and imply, for the actual members of the team?

It might be valuable, therefore, to examine the team approach as it works, within my own experience and in one particular residential setting. Two colleagues and I described the detailed working techniques and role of the hostel in question in a paper published some years ago.[1] Although, as a necessary framework

[1] *Parent, Child and Therapeutic Team in a Hostel Setting*, N. M. Gately, Joan Pollard and T. A. Ratcliffe. Case Conference Vol. 7, No. 4, September 1960.

for my comments, I must provide a brief preliminary note about the basic function of this hostel, I do not propose to repeat here the very detailed description which was given in that paper. My aim on this occasion is to consider how the roles of the various members of this particular therapeutic team interact with each other; and how this, in turn, affects their individual roles in, and with, the hostel.

This is a local education authority hostel which is an integral part of a long-established area child psychiatric—child guidance service. Its particular role is to work with difficult, rather than emotionally disturbed, children and adolescents within the school age range; and specifically for 15 children, including boys up to the age of 11+ and girls up to school-leaving age. Whilst the behaviour problem can be, and indeed often is, severe and considerable, we aim to select children (and this word is used here, and throughout, to cover the adolescent age-range also) who have some potential character on which to build; and from a family situation which has potential and concern also, but in which the behaviour problem has built up to such 'crisis' proportions as to be beyond the capacity of the parents to cope with at that stage. As I shall show, we pay particular care and attention in selecting the type of child, and problem, for which the hostel is designed; and therefore those children whom we can hope to help adequately.

When we come to analyse the therapeutic team in such a setting, we uncover (*inter alia*) two quite surprising facts—first, how large and complex the team is; and secondly in how many areas of day-to-day activity by the team, factors are operating which could be, at least potentially, dangerously disruptive to the team's unity. I felt that it would be valuable to discuss not only the complexity of this concept of a 'team'; but also the ways in which these disruptive threats can be, and indeed must be, circumvented. For greater simplicity I propose to examine these points separately as they appear in our selection procedures, and in the treatment situation once the child is in the hostel. It must be realized, however, that this is an artificial separation. The selection of those children who are suitable for our help, and the help which we actually give to them and their families during their period in hostel, in reality must form one total and indivisible process. For example, the initial assessment is the first contact which parent and child have with the therapeutic team; as such the impressions gained by 'both sides' during this preliminary stage will influence considerably the subsequent build-up of any therapeutic relationship.

As an agreed matter of policy, all the children are admitted to this hostel by, and through, the child guidance clinics of the two local authority areas involved. Because of the need to maintain close contact with the parents, we accept children only from a relatively limited geographical area. And, even when the child was initially seen at one of our other child psychiatric units or clinics, the final assessment for hostel is made at the child guidance clinic. As thc child psychiatrist concerned, and therefore the final member of the clinic's diagnostic team, it is my responsibility to make the actual professional decision on the child's suitability, or otherwise, for the hostel. It would be easy to see this as the end of the diagnostic process; and dangerously easy for me to say, in effect if not in actual words, 'the clinic's professional decision is that "X" must be admitted to the hostel'. But, even at this very early stage of our task, here is a situation which potentially could damage the whole team process. For there are still three members of the wider 'team' who must each play their vital role at this stage.

Quite apart from the suitability of 'X' for hostel treatment, there is the equally important decision to be made as to how far will he (or she) fit in with the current group of children in the hostel. Nor is this only a question of 'matching' the child by age or sex, important as this is. It is for the hostel staff to assess, and decide, how far this particular child, and behaviour problem, can be handled in the hostel at that particular time. For example, if a hostel is going through an unusually stressful period caused (let us say) by a series of recent abscondings, then the hostel staff may feel, and quite rightly feel, that it would be unwise and unfair to admit a child with similar problems at that particular time. Similarly, if there is a leaven of children already in the hostel who have progressed sufficiently far to be a stabilizing and positive factor, then the hostel will be able to accept, and help with, much more difficult problems than would be the case otherwise. All these are decisions for the hostel staff. Accordingly, at this stage of our assessment, and before any final decision is made, there must be a full discussion with the hostel matron. (In passing, may I stress that we dislike the title of 'matron' in such a setting; but we prefer it to 'warden' or 'superintendent'. In the absence of any better alternative, I will use it here.)

The pattern of my discussion with the hostel matron at this stage will illustrate some of the possible pitfalls; and how we try to avoid these. Our discussion will be informal, but full, open and entirely honest. However much I may feel that 'X' should go into hostel, it would be entirely wrong for me to 'sell' this plan by minimizing the size, or nature, of the problem; or by giving anything except a balanced and considered description of the situation. Equally the hostel matron, who is much more knowledgeable than I can be of the potential of her staff, and of the hostel group of children, will be just as honest and open in her approach. Each of us will view the decision from a different angle. However, this is a discussion between two people, each of whom is professionally trained and experienced in his or her particular field; and between two people who have been able to build up mutual respect for each other's skills and understanding. It is because there is this mutual trust and respect that we rarely, if ever, disagree in our final decision at this stage. But I would state quite categorically that, if our experienced hostel staff felt that a particular child was unsuitable for the hostel at that moment of time, I do not consider that it would be right, nor in the long-term interest of all concerned (including the child), to insist on any admission to the hostel at that point.

It may surprise some people to find that I am including the

parents as the next members of the therapeutic team. But with the type of child whom we have chosen to help at this particular hostel, the parents must become genuinely concerned throughout with the therapeutic process. To achieve this, we must be equally open and honest with the parents. Quite apart from my own discussion with the parents, it is our policy to invite the parents to visit the hostel, and meet with the hostel matron, before they make their final decision. (It goes without saying that the possibility of admission to hostel is discussed with the child at this stage also; but it would be outside the scope of the present lecture to discuss that aspect in any detail.)

In our meetings with the parents, we try to help them to see a hostel placement as a positive and constructive action; and we stress their own important role in helping the child. In addition, however, we give them a detailed account of the hostel regime and role, answering any of their questions fully and honestly. It is an interesting comment on how widely basic attitudes can differ, that, from time to time, some of my medical and administrative colleagues have queried the wisdom of such frankness with the parents at so early a stage. Some have been sceptical of whether we are as frank with the parents as we claim to be—and indeed are. We feel strongly, however, that, because the parental decision for their child to go into hostel is an entirely voluntary one, then it equally must be a 'genuine' agreement based on a knowledge of all the facts. Moreover, long experience has taught us that such honesty and frankness pays off in much more complete and continuing parental co-operation. Again, for reasons which will be obvious, most of our children are skilled, and often ruthless manipulators who, in the early stages after admission, will try hard to play off hostel against parent and vice-versa. It is far easier for both the parents and us to help over this difficult phase if the parents have this trust in the hostel. Finally, this involvement of the parents at this early stage has a considerable diagnostic and assessment value to us. Those parents whose principal wish is to 'offload' their child because of his nuisance value, or those who 'park' their child with us and show no real concern thereafter, will give indications of their basic attitude by declining to go through with a selection process which, after all, makes considerable demands on their co-operation from the beginning.

Once the parents, and we ourselves, have made a decision, there still remains one member (if, in the technical sense, a 'remote' member) of the team who must be consulted. Ours is an education authority hostel; and, as such, their formal consent to the child's admission must be sought. Here again is a possible disruptive situation. Any consultant is used to working in a hospital setting with charge of beds. In his hospital unit he can admit any patient whom he thinks appropriate, entirely on his professional responsibility, and certainly without seeking, or needing to seek, lay approval. He will find it difficult to see the reason for seeking such non-medical approval of his clinical decision before his patient can be admitted into the hostel. Moreover, when he has made this application, it is galling to receive a brief reply from some relatively minor member of the Education Department staff who says he 'sees no objection' to the child going into the hostel. It would be more than galling if this official *did* see some objection! But, to be fair, this has never happened to us. What the consultant must appreciate, however, is that there are valid legal and administrative reasons for this process. After all, if an authority is to spend money on what ranks as special educational help, then such financial commitment must be officially authorized. In return, of course, the authority must be willing to trust the clinical judgment of the rest of the team. For example, as regards this particular hostel, the authority has an agreed policy that they will admit children to the hostel *only* on the recommendation of the clinic and hostel team.

Once the child is in the hostel the same basic principles which I have described still apply; but the situation now is more complex. The hostel staff take on the major role of helping the child; and a new section of the team comes into the picture—the school which the child attends from hostel.

Our contact with the schools concerned is on several levels. The clinic already will have given the school the necessary factual information about the child: the name of the school which he had previously attended, his educational attainments and difficulties and so on. Where necessary during the child's stay in hostel, the appropriate member of the clinic team can pay a formal school visit. However, the chief links with the school lie with the hostel matron. In many ways she will be functioning as the 'good parent' *vis-à-vis* the school. She attends school functions just as a parent would. She is ready to back up the school when appropriate; but she can be as fiercely protective as any ordinary parent would be if one of her children is unfairly treated at school. She has, however, one great advantage in her contact with the schools which the average parent does not usually enjoy. She is likely to have four or five children at each of the schools concerned at any one time; and although the individual children will change, this will be a continuing contact over the years. As a result the school will learn what the hostel is trying to do, together with details of the limitations and possibilities of each individual child from the hostel. Equally the hostel matron will know the school, and its viewpoint. As a consequence, each can learn to trust the other; and to communicate with each other about the child. When we remember that we are dealing with very difficult, and ruthlessly manipulative, children, it is obvious that this good inter-communication between hostel and school staffs is of vital importance.

It would be outside the scope of our present topic to describe in detail the task of the hostel matron, although, at this stage, she has the most exacting, difficult and important role of any member of the team. We must consider, however, some particular areas of her work where there could be possible conflict within the team.

In any good residential setting, a complex and interlocking pattern of relationship should build up between the children and *all* those adults who are concerned with them in the unit. Each of these adults (and it must be remembered that the domestic as well as the hostel staff will be involved) will have an individual task within the structure and hierarchy of the hostel. Each will have a different place to fill in the total relationship needs of the children. Inevitably such differences, and the varying needs of individual children for differing adult relationships, can produce rivalries and jealousies between the adults concerned. Moreover, our particular type of child will not miss the chance to exploit such rivalries, and play off one staff member against the other. In welding these individual adults into a genuine team the hostel matron needs to be sensitive to these tensions; but secure enough in her own role to be able to cope with them.

The matron's role *vis-à-vis* the parents is also a complex one. For simplicity, we can consider this role from two particular angles. Her relationship and role with the children must be that of the 'good parent' (with all that this implies). Since, however, the whole aim of the hostel is to maintain good contact between parent and child, and to return the child to his own family relatively soon, the matron must not build up too strong, or too deep, a parental relationship with the child. She must see herself as the 'extra', rather than as the 'substitute' parent.

In every type of residential unit for children there will be areas where tension, mutual distrust and even open hostility can build up between parents and staff. The parental sense of guilt and failure, their mixed feelings when they see someone else 'succeeding' with a child with whom they have 'failed', are as potent and natural reactions as is the hostel staff's understandable feeling that the parents are 'to blame'. Once again, too, the ruthlessly manipulative child will exploit this situation; and there are many and obvious ways open to him (or her) to do just this.

One of the most commonly used techniques to limit and handle these tensions is to reduce the contact between residential staff and parents to a minimum; and to introduce a third 'neutral' person, usually a social case-worker, as the intermediary between parent and residential staff. The theory behind this policy, of course, is that the intermediary will be able to explain (or, if one wants to be technical, interpret) the tensions, difficulties and problems of each side to the other. Such a third person *can* have a valuable function; but only if two very important conditions are fully met. He (or she) must be a member of the therapeutic team in every sense of these words, with a close personal knowledge of, and contact with, the hostel staff, the hostel situation and the children concerned. Secondly, it is necessary to avoid the real risk that the intermediary and the hostel matron will be seen as, or feel themselves to be, rivals. No good residential worker worth her salt, and who is genuinely concerned with her task, would accept being 'frozen out' from any real and worthwhile contact with the parents. Indeed, in my view, she would be quite right to resent this. Moreover, whatever theoretical concepts and techniques we may quote, the parents will demand, and need, a good contact with that person whom they see as being closest to their child.

Our own carefully considered policy, developed over a number of years, is for the hostel matron to take a very full and important role *vis-à-vis* the parents, working in this role with either the psychiatric social worker or myself who act as the parallel, and additional, link with the parent. In very general terms, she will see the parents when they visit the hostel; and she is free to discuss with them any points which arise. Subsequently such interviews will be discussed fully with us; and if it is felt that some further action is advisable, then the psychiatric social worker or I will arrange to see the parents more formally at the clinic, or on a home visit. But this policy is kept very flexible. If, for example, such action is felt to be advisable at any time, the hostel matron and we will have a joint interview with the parents. During the holidays when the children are at home, it is the clinic section of the total team which maintains contact with parent and child.

In a hostel of this type, the child psychiatrist has a much more intimate, and frequent, contact with the children than he is likely to have in (say) a remand home or a children's department reception centre to which he is consultant. In these latter situations, his work will be mainly with the staff. In our hostel, I have a direct treatment role with the children themselves; and an indirect treatment role through the rest of the hostel staff. Since our form of treatment is what has been described as 'relationship' or 'environmental' therapy, it is a task in which both hostel staff and child psychiatrist will be involved equally. If such treatment is to be successful, we must work genuinely together; but there are areas where we can become jealous of each other—or even find ourselves in open rivalry. One such obvious area of possible rivalry, and one which the child certainly will exploit, is over disciplinary situations. For obvious reasons, most disciplinary (and other) decisions in the hostel will arise for, and be made by, the hostel staff. It must be remembered, too, that such problems are being handled within a day-to-day reality situation. For equally obvious reasons, the child psychiatrist will be greatly tempted to play the 'nice' parent; and to give way over, or even evade altogether, such disciplinary situations. Such action will certainly not help the child; but it will produce a very damaging and disruptive situation between the hostel staff and child psychiatrist. Moreover, just as the hostel matron is the 'additional mother', so the child psychiatrist, in this particular setting, must see himself as the 'additional father'. In that role he must involve himself (in the constructive sense of involvement) with all such problems, both with the child directly, and through his discussions with the hostel matron. Hostel matron and child psychiatrist must be genuinely and mutually supportive in this joint parental role.

It would be absurd to assume that all the members of the professional team will be in full agreement all the time. Indeed, it would hardly be a constructive situation if this were so. However, in discussing and working out their differences, the professional team members will be guided by a common professional ethic; and by a commonly held concern for the *genuine* welfare of the child and his family. Since one of the basic requirements of good group cohesion is the existence of a common goal, this is equally a source of strength towards the team's ability to work together in order to help the child in the best possible way.

Moreover, although the parents' motivation is personal, emotionally charged and not professional, they too will have this same desire for the child to be helped. If, therefore, those whose professional task it is to 'treat' the child can help the parent to see that there is this common goal between them, then parent and professional worker will become a team in the true meaning of that word.

The other side of this same coin can be seen in the difficulty which the officials of the local authority so often have in understanding what the hostel is really doing. This is not because they are deliberately unco-operative or unconcerned: but their professional ethic, and their role and goals, are quite different. It is not a question of the ethic and role of either side being right or wrong, or better or worse than the other. Nevertheless, if this difference is to be bridged adequately, there is a need for both sides to build up, by conscious effort, at least a common loyalty and trust; and, if possible, an insightful understanding of the differences between them.

There is, of course, a great deal more to the adequate and successful treatment of the child in a residential setting than the creation of a team which can genuinely work together; and there are many successful team patterns which would differ from ours. What we would contend is that unless, or until, such a team relationship is created, these other therapeutic techniques and aims will scarcely begin to get off the ground.

Chapter III

Truancy, School Phobia and School Refusal

School phobia most certainly exists as a clinical entity. Indeed, it represents one of the comparatively few real clinical emergencies of child psychiatric practice. A great deal has been written on this topic in the past ten years with Dr Kahn and Mrs Nursten's book[1] justifiably qualifying as the 'standard text-book' on this topic. It was the central theme of an NAMH Inter Child Guidance Clinic Conference some years ago; and even then (as the bibliography in the printed report[2] of that Conference shows), the published literature on school phobia was already extensive.

There is no doubt that the discovery and description of this syndrome has been, and indeed still remains, a most valuable contribution to child psychiatry; and one which has led to new therapeutic possibilities in cases of school absence. Nevertheless, we must retain our sense of proportion in assessing the value of this concept; for, as with any new product or important technical breakthrough, there is the very real risk that over-exploitation, or over-enthusiasm, can produce risks and dangers which finally outweigh the obvious advantages of the new discovery.

In the new products field, we have only to remember how the early over-use of penicillin for minor infections produced a situation where the micro-organism became so resistant to penicillin that its therapeutic value in serious infections was dangerously decreased. Similarly we are now beginning to recognize the dangers of drug-dependency when the tranquillizer group (products of undoubted value when used correctly) are

[1] *Unwillingly to School*, J. H. Kahn and J. P. Nursten, Pergamon.

[2] *Truancy—or School Phobia?* Report of an NAMH Inter-Clinic Conference, NAMH, London 1959.

prescribed too widely, and for conditions where such drugs are therapeutically valueless. In the mental health field, too, similar examples can be found. Few would deny that the work of Bowlby and his associates has been the major contribution in preventive mental health of the post-war period. However, its over-enthusiastic 'exploitation' in some quarters has not only enabled it to be discredited by some but, at the other extreme, has produced excessive and damaging parental anxiety and guilt-feelings over even brief, trivial and unavoidable mother–child separations.

Consequently, we need to consider school phobia in its relationship with the numerous other causes and types of non-school attendance. Otherwise there is a very real risk that school phobia will be used as the 'excuse' for *all* failures to attend school. Moreover, if we use therapeutic techniques which would be highly appropriate for true school phobia in a case of (say) truancy, our treatment may well do actual harm; and ultimately lead to destructive criticism of the value of these therapeutic methods in all cases. That this is a very real risk is well illustrated by recent correspondence in the journal *Education*.[1]

There are, of course, other factors which have increased this risk. As part of a general (if not always generally approved) trend towards a more 'permissive society', the official attitude and response to all forms of non-school attendance have changed appreciably during recent years. Whilst regular school attendance is still a statutory requirement, many education authorities have altered their basic policies towards its detection and enforcement. Indeed, one of the striking features is the wide variation between different authorities as to what constitutes a degree of school absence which requires notification by the school to the Education Department. In some areas an absence of more than a specified number of days without adequate and confirmed reasons has to be reported automatically; in other areas the school has a very wide range of individual discretion over reporting any absence of any duration. In many areas there are different rules as between

[1] *Education*, Issue of October 4, 1968, and subsequent issues.

junior and senior schools. There are similar wide variations in the action initiated by the education authorities. The policy of some authorities is to refer all cases of non-attendance at school to their school health or child guidance services; others prosecute the parents; others bring the child before the Juvenile Court. Some authorities appear to do nothing at all! It is tempting to assume that these different decisions and actions are a matter of arbitrary choice rather than that they are based on the needs of the individual case. What undoubtedly is a common factor in all these decisions, however, is that virtually all education authorities nowadays allow for longer periods of absence to elapse before initiating any action than was their policy formerly. In other words, there is a growing tendency to view absence from school as a much less serious matter. An interesting parallel development to this has been the change of role (and title) of the 'school attendance officers' into 'educational welfare officers'.

If, for the purposes of this discussion, we eliminate the 'legitimate' forms of non-school attendance (i.e. illness 'covered' by medical certificates, the whole family being away on their annual holiday and so on) we have remaining for our consideration three major types of absence from school. These three types, in fact, constitute the title of this lecture.

It is true, of course, that truancy, school refusal and school phobia form a continuum with considerable overlap between each of the three. Nevertheless, each one can be considered as a separate entity. And, as we shall see, each of the three must be recognized as a separate and distinct clinical condition of differing causation; and, therefore, requiring different treatment.

Of the three, truancy is the easiest both to define and to recognize. The central and characteristic feature of truancy is that it is a calculated action. There is a deliberate decision *not* to attend school. In virtually every case the decision not to go to school is made by the child. (In passing it should be noted that it is more likely to be the adolescent who truants, but the word 'child' is used throughout this lecture to cover the whole school-age range.) A second characteristic of truancy is that the failure to attend school has the implied or actual support of the parents. This degree of parental 'approval' may vary from active encouragement by the parents through to a complete lack of concern by them as to whether their child goes to school or not. It is not surprising, therefore, that truancy is more common in the social problem family which has a poor motivation towards, and limited cultural attitudes about, schooling. It is equally obvious that truancy will often be only one symptom in a lack of general supervision, social training or character development. Since, however, the basic decision to truant is made by the child himself, there will often be other contributory factors for his motivation to avoid school. The dull child, whose dullness has not been recognized and who is gaining nothing from school, is an obvious example of this. Similarly, the child whose general social training and adult interest or relationships have been defective will be more 'at risk' for truancy. Nor must we forget that the school (or school-class) which is unhappy, or of low morale, will have a higher incidence of truancy amongst its pupils. Just, as in a wartime Army the amount of absence-without-leave can be used as a valid yard-stick of unit morale and discipline, so the truancy rate can be used as one factor in assessing the 'quality' of a school—although in fairness to the school we must also consider the type of social population from which it draws its pupils.

Although it will be clear that possible school and educational problems must be investigated and, where necessary, rectified, the essential treatment of truancy lies in the field of constructive discipline and social training. It is very essential, therefore, that truancy be detected and dealt with at the earliest possible stage; and that whatever action is taken must be effectively carried through. Obviously, wherever possible, this constructive pressure should be put on the child with the willing co-operation (even if it is an 'assisted' or 'supported' willingness) of the parents; but it will be clear from what has been already said that this degree of co-operation may often not be achievable even with adequate support to the parents. It follows inevitably that, in an appreciable number of cases, legal action to bring the child before Juvenile Court will not only be necessary, but will be the action most genuinely in the long-term interest of the child. It follows, too, that a proportion of such children may require probation supervision over a long period, or committal to the care of the local authority.

There is a further characteristic of truancy which is important both in differentiating it from the other conditions which we shall be considering, and in determining the treatment needs which we have just described. Typically the truant has no sense of guilt and little concern over his behaviour. Although he may give plausible 'excuses', he makes surprisingly few efforts to conceal his actions or his motives. He works very much on the principle that he will not be found out—and if he is, that it was worth it!

School phobia is the very antithesis of truancy. It is much less frequently seen; it is virtually confined to adolescents, and most often of all to those of average or above average intelligence; and (with one proviso which will be described later) there is practically never any actual educational or school problem involved. But there are some even more significant and characteristic differences.

The child with school phobia *wants* to attend school. He (or probably rather more commonly in my experience, she) will drive himself desperately to continue to attend school until the pressure of his anxiety makes it impossible for him to achieve this. Even when this break occurs, there will be considerable guilt and anxiety over the non-attendance at school. As we shall see, this guilt is largely converted from deeper sources; but there is some direct guilt over the 'failure' to get to school. Equally, the parents will try hard to get their adolescent son or daughter back to school. Indeed, their drive to do so is very often excessive and guilt-driven. Linked with this sometimes excessive desire to attend school is the one occurring educational problem. A proportion of these children are self-driving; and their parents may have too high expectations for them. For some, therefore, the final precipitant is some apparent (as opposed to real) 'failure' at school. It should be emphasized, however, that this factor is the precipitant and not the cause of the condition. For the most important characteristic of school phobia is that the acute and severe anxiety, which is the classical symptom of this condition, stems from deeper unconscious sources. All these factors will have an obvious and vital influence on the treatment needs of the adolescent suffering from school phobia.

As I have already stressed, school phobia is an acute clinical emergency requiring urgent, and early, skilled psychiatric diagnosis and therapy. Far too often, if with the best of intentions, this acute condition is treated superficially or inappropriately before specialist help is sought. Distressingly often the child psychiatrist is not brought in for weeks, or even months, after the first absence from school. It is only fair to stress that this delay to refer the case is more often a failure of the medical, rather than of the administrative, services.

The unfortunate fact remains that, with such a delay, the problem will have 'hardened off'; and elaborate defence mechanisms will have been built up. Consequently, although the outlook for cases of school phobia treated early and adequately is good, the prognosis worsens rapidly and seriously with any delay in instituting therapy.

It would be outside the scope of this lecture to describe in detail the treatment of school phobia; but certain special features need to be mentioned here. Highly skilled psychotherapy for the patient, and equally skilled case-work with the parents, are absolutely essential. The acute anxiety often requires an intelligent use of the most appropriate form of sedation. To relieve the secondary guilt and anxiety, exclusion from school must be instituted at whatever stage the case is first referred. Indeed, school phobia is one of the few conditions which justify exclusion from school on psychiatric grounds alone. Having said this, however, it is equally important to stress that considerable professional skill will be required to judge the therapeutically correct moment to press for a return to school. Since this may have to be done gradually, or on a carefully observed trial and error basis, an appreciable proportion of such adolescent patients will need to be in a suitable residential unit, which has its own school attached.

Halfway along the continuum which we have described lies the third syndrome, school refusal. At each extreme it grades imperceptibly into school phobia and truancy; and it has been rarely described in the literature. Indeed, 'school refusal' is quite often used as if it were synonymous with 'school phobia'. Nevertheless school refusal is a clinical entity in its own right; and one which it is essential for us to recognize.

Although, as with other two conditions which we have described, school refusal is most often encountered in adolescence, its age spread is much the widest of the three. Characteristically, too, there is a long history of reluctance to attend school often dating right back into infant school days. There will be a similar long history of evasion of other situations which he, or she, has found difficult, or not wanted to face up to. Almost always the child will have built up a skilful and successful technique of manipulating the situation to his own immediate advantage. The school refusal, both in its motivation and pattern, will be another result of this weakly evasive, and narcissistically manipulative, technique. Typically there will be protestations, often dramatically stated, about the wish to return to school; but, unlike the sufferer from school phobia, this child will make no actual attempt to go back to school. There will be equally dramatic 'complaints' about school; but these complaints will be made without anxiety; and when challenged, the basic complaint will always 'boil down' to a dislike of school rather than to any specific difficulty there. Similarly, promises will be given to return to school if certain conditions—say a change of school—are met. Yet, even if these concessions are granted, fresh conditions, rather than an actual return to school, is the result. Basically, therefore, the problem is one of ego-weakness with some degree of inadequacy of character development.

It will not surprise us to find, therefore, that the parents of the child with school refusal will be unable, or unwilling (or both) to put positive pressure on the child towards his return to school. They may do this by 'covering up' for him through their own 'explanations' and 'excuses' for the non-attendance; they may be fiercely protective of their child; or they may react in other similar ways. We must remember, too, that although this parental attitude may stem from either 'over-loving' or 'under-loving', it will much more commonly arise from the former. In other words, the child-rearing pattern which leads to this type of problem, however damaging it must be for the child, will most often arise from the best of parental intentions. We could safely say, if in over-simplified form, that truancy is produced by the neglectful parent, but school refusal arises in the family with the 'too-good' parents.

One of the basic aims of much (but not, of course, all) of the therapy which we do with children is the provision, within the framework of a therapeutic relationship, of that component of parental relationship and experience which has been defective or missing. It follows from this, that whoever is to help the child exhibiting school refusal, will have to exert, within the framework of a therapeutic environment, that constructive support and understanding disciplinary pressure towards facing up to situations, which has not been the experience of the child in his home environment. The immediate aim of that pressure and support will be towards a speedy return to school; but it must be directed equally to every area of the child's life and activity (or lack of it). In other words, the treatment aim is to build up ego- and character-strength, with the return to school both as a therapeutic weapon, and as an essential step in this process.

If our pressure and support are to be constructive—or for that matter successful—these must be provided as firmly, as fairly, as confidently and at as early a stage as possible. As with school phobia, the prognosis rapidly worsens with delay, and with each 'failure' to achieve a return to school. We must assess the child's real potential so that we may push him into a situation with which we *know* that he can cope. And whilst we are very direct and firm in our pressure, we accompany it by our support, and by encouragement and approval as each forward step earns its reward. This is one of those not uncommon situations with children where 'respect' (an old-fashioned word, but one which still has a constructive meaning) is the first, and initially necessary, stage of an adequate therapeutic relationship.

Although this very direct help to the child is essential, it is equally necessary to modify the environmental factors also. Here again is a task for skilled case-work with the parents. Occasionally these parents will be actively unco-operative. Much more often they will be superficially most co-operative in terms of keeping appointments and so on, but unwilling, or unable, to accept any change in their own, or their child's basic attitudes. It is not surprising, therefore, that an appreciable proportion of these children do need a relatively long-term residential placement. Equally, there will be occasions when Juvenile Court action is necessary in the long-term interests of the child. It is worth commenting that, in a residential setting where school attendance is accepted as an entirely 'normal' event, most of these children return to school with no difficulty at all. Their feeling of achievement in doing this is a valuable, and valid, therapeutic tool.

Having discussed these three syndromes individually, we must now examine some important aspects of the three seen as a whole; and consider, too, the role of the child psychiatrist within this total problem.

Since not only the causation and symptomatology, but also the necessary treatment, differs so greatly between these three syndromes, it should be obvious that there is an urgent need for adequate and early professional diagnosis. In the case of school phobia, such skilled diagnosis is probably provided in most cases, even if that assessment is often too long delayed. But it is very doubtful if the same could be said of cases of truancy and school refusal.

It might be supposed that the existence of one common presenting problem of school absence between these three conditions would have made it easy for the child psychiatrist's differential assessment to be welcomed. But, in actual practice, two difficulties arise from this fact.

Although the child psychiatrist will willingly accept school phobia, and, to a considerable degree, school refusal as coming within his professional province, he is much less ready to see himself as having a professional role *vis-à-vis* the truant. Yet surely he *must* accept as part of his task the need for a skilled differential diagnosis even with the truant. If, however, the child psychiatrist continues to be reluctant to cover the whole field, this can only accentuate the other, and major difficulty. For absence from school is not just a symptom in the medical sense; it is also an administrative problem, and one which can have legal implications in addition.

Inevitably, therefore, the basic policy decisions, and indeed the final decision as to what is to be done in any individual case, will be made by the administrative authority; and not by the clinician. Without two-way and genuine co-operation and trust between clinician and administrator, it is clear that there will be a very real risk of serious conflict of aim and action between them. Such a conflict places the child psychiatrist in a particularly difficult and embarrassing position. For, in his normal consultant role within the 'medical' services, he is rightly used to taking sole and full professional responsibility for his advice and treatment. He is not accustomed to having his treatment decisions 'interfered' with by a lay authority. Since his professional duty is essentially to the patient, the child psychiatrist's attitude is both understandable and correct. The administrator would claim that he, too, has a responsibility, although a different one. Only when *both* sides to this potential conflict are genuinely prepared to understand each other's role and mutually to trust each other, will it be possible to provide the necessary adequate differential diagnosis and treatment which is the only long-term solution of this complex problem.

Chapter IV

The Three Generation Family

The considerable sociological changes which have affected many families in the past twenty years, have had more widespread effects upon the individual family than is perhaps always realized.

Nowadays there is a greatly increased tendency for people, and families, to move often quite frequently from area to area of the country. As a result the recently married couple may find themselves living a considerable distance away from their own parents, whereas in the past the 'larger family' of parents, grandparents, uncles and aunts and so on had tended all to live within the same general area of the home town.

One quite significant result of this is that when the children (and especially the first child) arrives, and later moves into and through early infancy, the young, and still inexperienced, parents do not have the grandparents to turn to for support and advice ('good' or 'bad'). This can have some advantages; but there are very real disadvantages also. On this occasion, however, we are to concentrate mainly on another aspect of this basic situation.

As the grandparents grow older, and particularly when one grandparent dies, leaving the other on his (or her) own, increased support for them will become necessary. When the larger family, including their own sons and daughters, lives nearby, this support and supervision often can be provided by frequent visiting. Moreover, when there are numerous sons and daughters, to say nothing of other relatives, this visiting does not place an undue, or continuous, burden on any one member of the family. But nowadays, with the much more prevalent situation of smaller families and wide geographical 'spread', it will be necessary in many more instances for the grandparent to live more or less permanently with one of their married children—and with the grandchildren, who, by this time, are probably moving towards, or into, adolescence. It is our task therefore to consider the problems, and strengths, of the three generation family in circumstances such as these.

Most of us like both to have our cake and to eat it; but grandparents are amongst the few people who are able to achieve this happy result with any regularity. This can be illustrated by the type of comment which one hears from the young mother who is telling her friends about the grandparents' attitude towards *her* children. 'The trouble is that *they* can overfeed Johnnie, or let him do just what he wants; but as soon as he is sick or troublesome they can literally pass the baby back to me!'

Whether spoken or unspoken, the underlying feeling behind such thoughts is obvious. When it is openly told to the grandparents (or to the child) the likely, and serious, repercussions are even more clear.

It is always difficult for parents to realize that their sons and daughters have *really* grown up. They know intellectually, of course, that their own children have reached the age of twenty, or twenty-five, or whatever it is; but the grandparents cannot entirely believe that their offspring have reached an age of discretion. Nor can they believe that their own sons and daughters are capable of handling their children as the grandparents think they ought to do; nor of running their household in the same efficient way as the grandparents run their own. A grandparent will often be reluctant to express such views outside the family; but, when actually face to face with the grown-up and married offspring, he (or is it perhaps more often she!) may vary from an indirect implication of criticism, to an open attempt to interfere with child-handling or house-management problems, in an advice-giving, or even direct, way.

It is tempting, and easy, to criticize this attitude; and to blame only the grandparent for it. It is an understandable reaction, however, since it is as children that they have longest known, and probably most loved, these newly grown-up young people. Besides, to admit this grown-upness in the next generation is to admit that they themselves have become middle-aged or elderly—and that is by no means an easy thing to do!

Moreover, the basic and normal responses of the middle generation itself can accentuate such attitudes in the grandparents. For, however strongly they protest against, or resent, any 'interference' by the grandparents, the younger married couple themselves may find it difficult to realize their own emancipation, and their new factual independence of parental 'authority'. It is not easy to be critical of one's own parents, without some feelings of guilt; nor is it easy to disregard their advice, especially when one remembers that, in the past, one was only too ready and willing to turn to them for advice and support over one's own childhood troubles and worries. This is particularly true if a relative inexperience in the skills of parenthood and housekeeping makes the younger parent still secretly feel as worried, and as much in need of support, as they ever felt during their own childhood.

Inevitably, two important and interrelated results will emerge from all this. Mutual support between older and the younger generation can be, and should be, a positive force. But to attempt to replace mutual support by a dependency-domination attitude is to court disaster. The younger parent who is still too dependent on the older generation cannot mature into adult parenthood in his own right. Equally, the grandparent who attempts too obviously, or too powerfully, to dominate the situation will provoke, at best, open rebellion; or, at worst, an impossibly chaotic set of standards and loyalties for all concerned—and most of all for the grandchildren. When such chaos rules, the child will find it difficult or impossible to establish his own standards, or feel secure. Such inconsistency of handling from the important adults in his world will be exploited to the full, and to his own advantage, by any normal child. Such shrewd manipulation ruthlessly applied by the child, as it will be, must strain adult loyalties, and accentuated existing differences and difficulties between parents and grandparents.

What is probably of even greater importance is that when a child, and even more an adolescent, learns how to achieve 'success' (in however a short-term and self-centred sense of that word) by playing one adult off against another, he will quickly develop and use these same manipulative techniques in other situations outside his home. At best this will produce considerable behaviour and handling problems with, and for, him; at worst it will seriously impair his maturation and character development.

Nevertheless, it would be well-nigh impossible for these two different adult generations to see eye-to-eye over every child-rearing situation. For reasons which will be clear from our earlier comments, it is normally easier to use realistic techniques of child handling, and insist firmly on reasonable standards, when that same person has the responsibility of coping also with the immediate, and long term, results of those techniques in comparison with the situation when that individual sees the child for only brief periods, during which one can allow (temporarily) greater freedom and less definite standards with the child.

As we have stressed already, the expectations and degree of toleration of specific behaviour will vary as between the older and the younger adult generations. 'I never behaved in that way when *I* was young' is a frequent and understandable battle-cry of any older generation; and as any adolescent with whom you have a good enough contact will tell you, it is a comment which is very difficult to counter! Moreover, there is an important variant to be considered in the circumstances with which we are here concerned. For, in criticizing some action by the younger parents towards their children, the grandparents will often comment: '*We* never treated you in that way when you were a child.' Now, often enough, this may not be a true comment; and the younger parents may know that it is not true. Nevertheless, this fact will increase, rather than lessen, its impact on them.

There will always be a 'generation gap', as again any parent with an adolescent boy or girl can tell you. But, in the three-generation family, there will be two such gaps. It will be obvious that this must produce additional complications. Equally obviously, it must make the total generation gap between grandparent and grandchild very wide indeed. Moreover, although such a gap must have been present at every stage of western civilization, recent and much more rapid technological and cultural changes inevitably have resulted in a still wider gap of knowledge, experience and opportunities as between any two generations.

When the grandparents are only occasional visitors to the home of the young parents, such differences of attitude, standards and expectations may cause little serious difficulty. The regime of the household can be modified for the period of the stay to suit the grandparents. Allowances can be made by all concerned for a short period. The physical strain on the grandparents, faced with the natural lively behaviour of a young child, may not be a serious problem if their stay in the household is relatively brief. Obviously, however, the problem will be very real when the three generations actually live together in the same house virtually on a permanent basis and with little prospect of 'relief' from the existing situation. That is to say, in the circumstances with which we are here concerned.

In such a setting, very considerable strains will be put upon the loyalties—and the tempers and reactions—of all concerned. Often such strains will appear most vividly over everyday incidents and decisions. Should Angela, the fifteen-year-old daughter, *never* have her teenage friends in for a pop-session when her grandfather is well known as disapproving of such music, or indeed of any noisy activities. Or should the grandmother's long-established practice of having a rest after tea involve seven-year-old Kevin in *always* being very quiet at that time?

There can be no complete or perfect 'solution' to such situations; and no absolutely 'right' or 'wrong' decision. Yet such decisions will have to be made, and such solutions found, day after day and often in a 'crisis' situation. Mutual loyalties must be balanced, and kept in balance.

Perhaps, however, 'solution' is not the most appropriate

word here; and there will be both 'right' and 'wrong' on both sides of the argument. What is much more important (and more possible) than an actual 'solution' is the family 'atmosphere' in which that solution is made; the degree to which there can be any genuine and understanding give-and-take; the way in which the essential and differing needs of parent, grandparent *and* child are all considered and allowed for.

It is tempting to consider only the needs, or worse still only the demands, of the children in such a family situation. Certainly their future development, as well as their immediate contentment and security, are very much at stake. Any good family will, and should, aim to provide the best environment possible for their children. It is essential to remember, however, that a 'good' environment will not be created if that environment is entirely 'child centred'. The opportunity to play and to learn, to behave at one's own level and to gain experience of life, are all essential requirements for any child or adolescent; but so are a gradually increasing ability to accept necessary frustrations and an ability to fit in with the needs and demands of other people in one's environment.

As we have seen, the three-generation family may increase the stress; but if these problems can be successfully overcome, then the end result will be both a happy family atmosphere and an increased ability to cope more maturely with other stresses in other situations outside the family.

Chapter V

The Problems of Normal Adolescence

It may seem unusual to begin a lecture by drawing the audience's particular attention to its title. Very often the only function of the title which is chosen for a lecture is to indicate the general theme on, and around which, the lecturer will be speaking. In this present instance, however, I have chosen the title with particular care and thought. For it indicates clearly the central, and essential, point which I wish to make, namely that, although adolescence is a period of stress which produces problems both for the teenager and those adults who have a responsibility for his welfare and upbringing, it is an inevitable and necessary part of the normal process of growth, maturation and development.

In recent years there has grown up a 'mystique' about adolescence as though it were some new and hitherto unrecognized phenomenon. The teenager, although certainly not by his own choice, is placed on a pedestal as a unique object who is to be venerated, given way to in all matters and treated with circumspect care; or, at the other extreme, he is condemned as being anti-social, constantly in a state of aggressive rebellion against any form of authority, and very prone to sexual promiscuity, drug-taking and the like.

It is perfectly true, of course, that, as with any other age-group, there are adolescents to whom these criticisms of 'anti-social' behaviour do apply. There has been an increase in the number of illegitimate births to young girls, and in the drug-addiction and VD incidence-rate for this age range. Similarly the number of adolescents appearing before Juvenile Court is considerable.

Yet even if we add all these facts and figures together, it would hardly justify the condemnation of a whole generation; or indicate that *all* teenagers fall into these anti-social categories. Moreover, there are a number of fallacies in the facts and figures themselves; and these are rarely mentioned. For example, if we are to be entirely fair, we ought to balance the increase in the incidence of these anti-social episodes against the increase of the total population within this age-range. Then again, the most frequently quoted figures for drug-taking, illegitimate births and the like usually include such incidents occurring not only in adolescence but in the eighteen plus to twenty-one 'young-adult' group also. Finally, and perhaps most significantly of all, any anti-social episode by any teenager tends to be given maximum publicity and comment; much less mention is made of the larger proportion of adolescents who mature through, and cope with, this period of change with no major damage to themselves or to others.

I have stressed these points at some length for, as a child psychiatrist, one sees how often, and how greatly, the parental and adult attitude towards their teenage charges (and adolescents in general) is governed by apprehension, uncertainty and hesitation bred of this 'social' attitude towards the problem. It is my hope, therefore, to indicate that the vast majority of teenagers, including those who have difficulties or who are difficult, are in fact essentially 'normal'; and that in general the adolescent is a very rewarding, and surprisingly easy, person to help towards satisfactory maturation.

To say all this is not to deny that there are problems for all concerned during this period. Indeed, this must be so, since this age-range of twelve to seventeen is a time of major and inescapable change from childhood through into adulthood. Changes of this sort, and indeed any changes in ourselves or in our environment, are a vital and unavoidable part of the processes by which we mature, evolve and gain from experience. Nevertheless, such changes are also periods of increased stress and difficulty for us. Adolescence represents a very major change, and one which is gradual, unavoidable and involving physical, social and emotional readjustments in virtually every area of life.

There is a further general factor which we must consider at this stage, if we are fully to appreciate the problems of normal adolescence. Although the phrase 'the generation gap' is a modern one, if we look back into history we will find evidence also not only of the existence of such a gap, but of the mutually critical (and criticizing) attitude which went, and goes, with this generation gap. The reasons for this long-standing and basic attitude are not difficult to find. To the adult, the teenager must represent the up-and-coming generation, the rival, and the person who will shortly be threatening the adult's place in the world. Moreover, this 'threat' appears most often when the parents themselves are moving into middle-age, a stage of equally great adjustment difficulty for them; and a period when they are increasingly vulnerable to any reminder of their own advancing years.

It is in the light of these 'normal', but nevertheless considerable, background problems that we must now try to analyse the difficulties which the teenager himself faces; and the difficulties which he produces in, and for, the adult world of parent, teacher and the like.

It ought to be obvious, although it is very often forgotten, that the adolescent is neither a child nor is he an adult. Certainly his life experience as a child will greatly influence the pattern of his adolescence, just as what happens to him as a teenager will mould him into the sort of adult which he is to become. But to think of him, or to try to handle him, as either adult or child is to miss the essential point of his adolescence. To quote Keats on this subject, adolescence is

> 'The space of life in between in which the soul is in a ferment, the character undecided, the way of life uncertain.'

Or, as any teenager might sum it up, there are those two recurring adult admonitions which seem so mutually contradictory: 'You're not old enough to do that' and 'You're old enough to know better'.

At first sight the pattern of normal adolescence appears to be both complex and confusing; but, in fact, most of the various adjustments and happenings of adolescence can be described under three separate, but still interrelated, sets of events.

Although it is true to say that, throughout the whole of childhood, the child's 'world' is an ever-expanding one, this enlargement of his environment and experience, physically, emotionally, educationally and socially, becomes much more rapid and dramatic during adolescence than it has been at any stage since early infancy—which, in its way, was an equally important and similar period of major adjustment. Educationally he (or, as throughout this lecture, she) will be now in senior school with its new demands and interests and its new techniques of learning. Socially and culturally, he will be moving into new, wider and different relationships with his own peer group, with adults and with the opposite sex. There will be new opportunities, as well as new risks and new prohibitions, to cope with.

Like all of us in similar circumstances, the teenager has a natural and powerful desire to explore his expanding world and to 'experiment' with these new opportunities. But this rapid expansion of the adolescent's world is neither matched nor equalled by a corresponding increase in his basic experience of life. Inevitably, therefore, the teenager will not, and indeed cannot, know which new experience is safe to explore, or dangerous: which new opportunity will prove profitable or the reverse: or which activity will be socially acceptable or disapproved of by the adult world.

It should not surprise us, therefore, that virtually every teenager from time to time must indulge in behaviour which appears foolish and inappropriate. But, much more importantly, every adolescent faced with these frequent new, unknown and untried situations will feel unsure, doubtful how to proceed, and anxious. For the teenager, therefore, there is an intensification of that basic conflict between what one can do and cannot do, and between what one would like to do and what one should not attempt. Moreover, not only is this conflict itself intensified, but its solution is made much more difficult and unsure by the adolescent's lack of experience in these new and particular areas.

The second major factor and event which characterizes this age period is closely linked to the one which I have just described; and, as we shall see, each greatly accentuates the other.

Obviously, no normal child always does what he is told: and there must be occasions when he cannot, and does not, accept parental judgments and decisions. Nevertheless, when there is any sort of adequate adult–child relationship, the young child basically accepts parental authority; and sees, and trusts, the adult figure as infallible, all-knowing and always reliable. But with the onward growth and development of adolescence there comes a questioning of adult authority, and a doubting of adult infallibility. This is an inevitable reaction; and, indeed, it is a necessary part of the process of maturation into adulthood. The real problem arises because this child–adult bond and trust is weakening just at the very moment when the teenager most needs to have this 'reliable' and 'trusted' adult to be available to him. Or, to change the analogy, it is as if someone is being asked to embark on a voyage into a new sea for which he has no charts; and when, moreover, his previously good compass is now more difficult to read, and apparently no longer as reliable as it was.

Once again, we should not be surprised to find unsureness, anxiety and 'difficult' behaviour as common reactions in the adolescent. Equally we should not be surprised to discover that the characteristic adult–teenager relationship includes an intensely strong, but unsurely applied, need to keep that relationship bond as secure and as strong as possible. In terms of reality, this explains why the adolescent's attitude to the adult (and particularly to the parent) so often is unsure, or provocative or apparently rebellious. It explains, too, why so much teenager behaviour and reaction is manipulative and 'trying-out' in type. After all, his urgent need is to find out just how secure and mutually trusting that relationship can be in his newly found situation. In all this, there is an obvious element of rebellion, and a desire to escape to personal independence—as is most natural and necessary; but it is essential that we recognize also the equally important fact that the teenager is making demands for continuing adult guidance, and even for some continuing adult authority and external control. Although, in adolescence, the techniques used are more sophisticated and more calculated, one is very much reminded of those reaction patterns of late infancy by which, for similar basic reasons, the small child battles through an acute phase of the conflict between his desire for both freedom and control. With both the infant and the teen-ager we have to remember always that much of their provocative, demanding and difficult behaviour is motivated by a need and desire to discover the definite and firmly fixed boundaries of acceptable behaviour. If we do not remember this, and provide such necessary boundaries in each case, it is not surprising that the degree of anxiety, and of provocative behaviour, will increase.

The third major problem of adolescence which we must now consider stems from the fact that this is a period of marked physical growth and change. Moreover, these bodily changes are both inevitable and obvious to all concerned. Whether the teenager (or for that matter, the parent) want it or not, there *is* a physical change into adulthood; and its signs, such as hair-growth, changes of voice and body contour and the onset of menstruation, cannot be hidden, disguised or side-stepped. In theory, all these are factors which need not produce embarrassment but in practice almost always do so. Even in the best adjusted families, at this stage one will see that characteristic mixture of excessive modesty and provocativeness over these early signs of physical and sexual development.

Even more important, however, is the fact that these physical changes will be accompanied by an equally unavoidable, powerful, new and entirely different emotional reaction towards the opposite sex. In analytical terms, this is a re-awakening of the basic oedipal conflict which, whether solved or unsolved, has been relatively dormant during the period of latency. In reality terms, it is a particularly dramatic and important expansion of the teenager's 'world'.

Clearly the nature and depth of any emotional disturbance at this point will be determined by the success, or otherwise, with which the original oedipal conflict was resolved. But, again put in reality terms, it means that the first impact of this developing adult sexuality will be on the adolescent's relationship with the parents, and particularly with the parent of the opposite sex. If the teenage boy cannot work through his new emotional feeling for his mother without excessive guilt, or if the adolescent girl cannot successfully, naïvely and, above all, safely 'flirt' with father, then difficulties can arise; difficulties which not only produce immediate problems over the parental relationships but will handicap the further development of those more sophisticated social and sexual needs which will come later. We have here another illustration of the way in which each of the adjustment situations of adolescence are inter-linked. For this urgent need for an emotional bond between parent and adolescent occurs just at the point where each (if for different reasons) is demanding a greater independence from the other, and where the old secure, mutually trusting relationship no longer feels so safe or certain as it did.

There are, of course, many other 'normal' problems of adolescence which need to be considered; but we have time to touch only briefly on some of these.

Maturation is never a regular, or entirely predictable, process; nor does it occur at the same rate in different individuals. The progress of development, whether physical, emotional or social, will vary greatly, although still within 'normal' limits, in any group of (say) fifteen-year-olds whom one selected. Moreover maturation does not keep in step with itself in the various areas of development even in any one individual. In terms of physical development alone, very many adolescents have reached adult maturity by fifteen or sixteen years of age. Their emotional and social development, and their experience of life, has not kept pace with this physical progress, however, whilst necessary economic, cultural and legal factors must prevent them from assuming a fully adult role in the world at this stage. Inevitably, and indeed wisely they still must make different adjustments in these various areas of life.

So far, we have been considering mainly the impact of these various problems upon the teenagers themselves; and it was important that we should have started our study from the adolescent's own angle, since it is they who have to achieve the necessary degree of maturation. However, we must not fall into the error (which nowadays is so widespread) of considering only the adolescent boy or girl; or of visualizing him or her as almost a separate social species, isolated from the adult world and requiring only contact with their own peer group to settle every teenage problem. Yet no individual, and no social group, could exist in such isolation. Whatever generation-gap there is, the adult, and particularly the parents, are a vital and necessary part of the teenager's world; and if it is to be wholly successful the parent–adolescent relationship must be 'two-way', in every sense of that phrase. It is essential, therefore, that we should consider now the impact of these adolescent problems on the adults concerned; and consider too how best those adults who are closest to the teenager can help to make his or her maturation and adjustment as happy, and as successful, as possible.

The first major pitfall which must be avoided by the concerned adult (and there is a subtle, but important, distinction to be made between the 'concerned adult' and the 'adult concerned with' the teenager) whether as parent, teacher, youth-leader or whatever, is that he will abdicate, partly or wholly, from his adult role of responsibility. No adolescent will be helped by, or respond to, an adult who tries to be a pseudo-teenager himself. For one thing the adult will not, and indeed cannot, succeed in playing this role adequately or successfully; and, in the second place, the adolescent wants, and needs, him to be a 'genuine' adult. But what sort of adult, or parental, figure does the teenager actually need?

Quite a good starting-point for answering this question would be to consider the real significance of the two words—'trust' and 'respect'—words whose meanings are quite often diminished, and even discredited, in this day and age. But mutual trust, and mutual respect, are both necessary components of the adult–adolescent relationship. As the additional word 'mutual' implies, such trust and respect must be a two-way process. Each side must be able to trust, and to respect, the other. Which means, of course, that both the trust and the respect must be earned. Each side must learn to understand and value, but not necessarily accept or agree with, the other's viewpoint, needs and ideas.

We have already seen how much the teenager wants, and needs, to achieve this goal; and the difficulties which he will find in trying to achieve it. It will therefore often be necessary for the adult, and especially the parent, to take the initiative. How can this best be done? And why do so many parents find it so difficult to achieve this initiative, and good relationship, with the adolescent?

A certain number of parents see the solution as continuing to treat the teenager exactly as they did when he, or she, was a child. They can attempt to achieve this in one of two ways: either by maintaining the same controls and restrictions as were considered suitable in childhood; or they may over-protect the adolescent to avoid him having to face up to any of the new 'risks', or new situations and stresses, of adolescence. By neither of these means will the adult or the teenager achieve mutual trust or respect for each other. The result, at best, will be open rebellion; and, at worst, there will be a serious and damaging failure to mature.

The other, and much more common, error is to assume that the teenager is already an adult, with the adult's maturity, skills, experience and wishes. Here the parent withdraws from his adult responsibility, and provides no adequate support, control, interest or guidance, leaving *all* the decisions to the adolescent. There are, of course, two possible basic motivations for this sort of parental attitude. For the unconcerned, the uninterested, and the self-centred parents, this technique represents the 'easy way out', and one which makes little or no demands upon the adult. But a very similar pattern of parental response can be much more positively, if still unwisely and mistakenly, motivated. The 'good parent' who tries too hard to be 'understanding', who is afraid of 'hurting' or 'repressing' the teenager, or of losing his love, may easily become over-permissive and, in the way which we have just described, be equally abdicating from his or her parental task.

Nevertheless, whether the parents act in this way with the best of intentions, or because they do not wish to bother themselves to do otherwise, the result must be to lose the adolescent's trust and respect, replacing these by increased anxiety, uncertainty and difficult behaviour in the teenager. For, as I have tried to demonstrate already, the central problems of adolescence stem from the desire to grow up and the risks of doing so, and from the uncertainty as to what one can (or should) do, and what one cannot (or should not) do. The adults' and the parents' true role must be to provide a stable and secure framework, and to lay down with confident and understanding firmness where the boundaries of acceptable behaviour and action lie. Within, and knowing of, such boundaries, the teenager will feel secure enough, confident enough and free enough to experiment safely and successfully with the immediate problems of growing up. Obviously, these boundaries will have to be set now much more widely than was the case in childhood; and the boundaries must be modified appropriately to match the maturity (or lack of it) in the individual teenager at that particular time. To use a different analogy, the 'rope' which we let the adolescent have must be long enough; but not so long that he hangs himself. Moreover, and this is the vital point, it must be the adult who finally determines the length of the rope. It is, of course, this need to make such firm decisions, and insist upon them, which saps the confidence of so many otherwise willing and concerned parents and adults. As a consequence, the parent may be tempted to give up the task altogether; or to impose the boundaries of acceptable behaviour so unsurely, or unjustly, or with so little confidence, as to be both valueless and unacceptable to the adolescent.

If, however, the parents are to be able to carry through their vital, but difficult, role *vis-à-vis* their adolescent sons and daughters, or if we are to help them to do so, then it is essential that they, and we, recognize and appreciate the many factors which make it so difficult for the parent to do this task successfully.

It will be clear from my comments so far that, to be successful, the parents must believe in, and feel confident about, the standards which they are setting for, and demanding of, the teenager. This implies that the parents must be equally certain of their own personal standards. Nor is such a confident belief so common, or so easily reached, as it was in the past. There is nowadays far less acceptance of basic conventions and ethical standards. There is a small, but very vocal, minority of people who insist that absolute freedom, and the absence of any controls or restrictions, represents the only possible way of life; and who have a far greater influence on adult, than on adolescent, thinking and attitudes. There are, too, the very strong 'commercial' pressures from those who (with some practical justification) see this adolescent generation as a relatively wealthy group, and therefore a profitable market to exploit. They try to set quite different standards and expectations for the teenager. Their skilled use of advertising techniques can, and often do, place both parent and adolescent under considerable pressures, although clinical experience suggests that the 'ideal world' which they present is not the type of world that most adolescents would choose for themselves without such pressures.

Finally, and probably most important of all, there is the difficulty of communication between the two generations. For, although this difference is often seen as greater than it is in reality, there are many occasions where the parent can miss, or misinterpret, the teenager's methods of communication, especially if it is forgotten that the adolescent, like the child, more often 'acts out' than talks about his real needs and problems; and that virtually every adolescent reaction and activity has a manipulative or dramatic element to it. Let us look at some everyday examples.

The fifteen-year-old girl who says (as she quite often will) 'It isn't fair. All the other girls in my class are allowed to do that. Why can't I?', will provoke guilt and uncertainty in any good parent—

unless the parent recognizes that this is the motive for the remark, and that it was never intended to be a statement of fact. Sulking and moodiness and rather infantile tempers are not uncommon, but these are almost invariably a transient immature reaction, or a skilfully timed manipulative weapon; and very rarely indeed an indication that the teenager feels himself unloved or unwanted. Similarly we should not assume that all difficult behaviour is always evidence of overt rebellion against authority. Quite frequently it will be an attempt to get someone in authority to be firm, and to lay down definite standards and boundaries. Even when the behaviour is really serious, or highly dramatic, the same may still be true. If we consider what is one of the most alarming behaviour episodes of all—running away from home—there still will be many possible alternative motives for this action. It is true, of course, that some children do run away because they are deeply unhappy at home; but this is probably the least common cause of all. For some others it will be an impulsive 'adventure', or an attempt to prove (to oneself rather than to others) that a certain level of maturity has been reached. Sometimes it will be done to avoid the consequences of some delinquent episode. But most often of all it will be a provocative act of bravado, or the result of some temporary upset, when it is really no more than a very dramatized pattern of sulking. Or it may be a 'cry for help'. Perhaps, therefore, this particular piece of behaviour illustrates better than any other how often, and in how many ways, the teenager acts out his reaction to some immediate, and quite often relatively superficial, reality situation. It illustrates equally vividly the vital need for an accurate understanding of the real meaning of adolescent behaviour seen as a technique of 'communication'. After all, the ability to handle any such situation to the real benefit of all concerned must depend on an accurate assessment and understanding of what that episode of behaviour really implies.

If all this sounds extremely difficult, it is still no more than what the good parent has been trying to do and, very often, has succeeded in doing, throughout the whole of their offspring's infancy and childhood. The real difficulties only arise if we see our teenaged son or daughter as somehow 'abnormal', or unmanageable, or dangerously rebellious or unalterably non-communicative with us; or if we confuse discussion with argument; or, most of all, if we see our teenager as so 'explosive', or so easy to damage, that we are afraid to tackle any situation with him or her.

Which is just another way of saying that, if we have laid a good foundation with them in infancy and childhood, if we know what adolescence (and adolescents) are about, if we have a genuine liking for teenagers and if we are ready to hold a just balance between freedom and control, then we shall find this age group almost the most rewarding and responsive of all.

Above all, we shall have helped them to grow through to maturity, to adequate self-discipline and to adulthood. And that, after all, is the whole purpose of the exercise.

Chapter VI

On Working with Young People

One of the most striking features to be found amongst those who work in the field of education is the enthusiasm, and frequency, with which they seize upon new ideas as these arise. This practice represents one of the great strengths of the educational system; but it can also be the source of one of its greatest potential weaknesses. The problems arise because such new ideas and concepts are introduced too often on a basis of enthusiasm, rather than of adequate research. There is, too, a tendency (from which the Department of Education and Science, and even the Secretary of State, do not appear to be immune) to assume that anything which is new *must* be an improvement on the old, just because it is new. Of course, I do not wish to deny the real value of many new developments in educational practice; but I would stress that there is always a need to study carefully both the values *and* the limitations of all such new projects.

One comparatively recent development in this field, and one which has raised considerable interest and enthusiasm, is the concept of 'youth counselling'. There are a number of different ways in which this task is envisaged. The concept of the professionally trained school counsellor came to us from the United States. From this source, the current dispute has arisen as to whether the school counsellor could, or should, be a teacher also. In addition, we must remember that such professional skilled counselling tasks fall also within the province of some agencies which already exist—the child guidance clinic for example. I do not propose to discuss in any detail here the various, and important, advantages and disadvantages as between a professional counselling service within the school itself, and one provided by a 'non-school' organization. However, I am myself, understandably enough, but for a variety of sound technical reasons also, strongly in favour of the latter method.

I do not propose to attempt the impossible task of describing, in one short lecture, the detailed techniques of professional counselling. Understandably enough, however, there are many other people working in close contact with children (and most notably of all teachers and youth leaders) who quite rightly see themselves as having a part in this task of counselling. Many such people have already sought guidance and training on how best they can help with the personal, social and emotional problems of those adolescents who are under their care, but without attempting to make use of the full technical skills of the professional counsellor. It is with this type of what might be called 'para-counselling' help that I am particularly concerned here.

There are four main areas which must be considered if we are to learn how best to carry out this task—the nature and quality of the relationship; the degree of emotional involvement (or otherwise); the way in which any such help should be related to the reality situation; and the ability of the helper to listen understandingly, as well as to provide guidance. I have quoted these factors in what I feel to be their order of importance; but, of course, all four are closely inter-related. It will be simpler, therefore, to discuss these in a rather different order.

It is tempting to see the task of helping over some particular problem as though such help must be confined only to that particular occasion and problem. It is true that, for the professional therapist or counsellor, the crisis itself may be the first opportunity for contact with the client. But the teacher, the youth leader, and so on, usually will have the great advantage of a prior and continuing contact, so that helping over this specific crisis is only part of a much wider task. The benefits which arise from such previous contact are two-fold. It will have given an opportunity to make the first steps towards, or even fully to develop, a relationship between helper and helped. Such a relationship can be built up spontaneously within the reality situations of ordinary day-to-day contact. In such a setting the adult can show, and 'prove', himself to be reliable, understanding, trustworthy and just (or otherwise) by his handling of these everyday situations. By these means he can reach that necessary starting point for helping anyone, namely the client's acceptance of him as someone from whom an individual under stress can safely and usefully seek help. On the other hand, if in his previous contacts the adult has shown himself to be over-anxious, or indecisive, or unfair, or unable to keep his promises, or if he has demonstrated in any other way his inadequacy as an adult, then it should not surprise us if the adolescent does not turn to such a person at his moment of crisis. The positive benefits of this pre- and post-crisis relationship will be apparent in other areas too. For, quite apart from his help over any specific 'crisis', the adult can do a great deal to aid in the maturation and adjustment of the adolescent by his reaction to, and with, the ordinary day-to-day situations of school or youth club. In other words, in our enthusiasm for counselling and for helping over any crisis situation, we should never forget our equally important task of giving our teenager an increasing capacity to cope successfully with the stresses and strains which inevitably must appear during his life experience.

Moreover, it is only when this good, basic and continuing contact exists that the teacher or youth leader is likely to notice, or to recognize, the crisis when it actually does 'blow up'. Many adolescents do not make an open, or direct, request for help. Much more often the worker must be able to recognize the dramatic but usually indirect 'cry for help' which indicates the presence of such a crisis. In passing, we should remember also that we shall only recognize the crisis if we really *want* to do so. The major factors in our willingness, or otherwise, to do just this stem from our own personality, with its resistances and prejudices: but if we already have an existing and positive relationship with the teenager, then we are more likely to want to help over, and therefore to notice, the existence of the problem.

It must be obvious from all these points that the teenager seeks our help not solely because we are the teacher, the youth leader, the counsellor or whatever, but mainly because we have earned the trust of the adolescent and proved our willingness and ability to help him. I have described already some of the ways in which we earn that trust before the crisis breaks. We must now consider in what ways we best sustain this trust, and strengthen our relationship, once our help has been sought over the specific problem.

The first, and completely essential, requirement of course, is a genuine concern for people, and for the person under stress in particular. The important word here is 'genuine', for no amount of false sympathy or synthetic interest will be of value. Equally, neither a cold detached attitude, nor an intense personal involvement in the problem, can create that genuine 'atmosphere' of trust which is required. Perhaps the most difficult part of our task is to achieve this necessary, but critical, balance between over- and under-involvement.

When we have a problem of our own to cope with, one of our major handicaps will be that we do not, and indeed cannot, view the problem in proper perspective, or with any sort of objectivity. We are, in fact, so emotionally tied up with our problem that we cannot see the wood for the trees, or even begin to sort out any sort of possible solution. Moreover, if we seek 'advice' from all our friends—and most of us do this on such occasions—the very varied advice and suggestions which we shall receive can make us more confused than ever on how to solve the problem. If this is true of an adult in such circumstances, it is doubly true of the adolescent, who must have even less basic experience on which to base his solution.

It is obvious, therefore, that if we are to help the teenager through a period of stress and crisis, we ourselves must be able to remain sufficiently detached from the problem so that we, at least, can remain objective; and thus be able to use that objectivity to help the adolescent towards an ultimate solution of his problem. If, however, we become as involved as our client is, then we are in no better a position to help him than he would be to help himself.

At the other extreme, there is the story of the eminent zoologist who was on safari in Africa with his family. One day, when he was in his tent writing up his notes, his wife arrived to tell him agitatedly, 'Come at once, one of our children has fallen into the river and is being attacked by an alligator'. To which the zoologist replied, 'Surely you know by now that there are no alligators in Africa, but only crocodiles'. This was the height of scientific non-involvement—but it was of no great help, or support, to those in distress! In other words, there is the equally great danger of our being so coldly detached that we fail to provide any feeling of support or understanding to those who have sought our help.

We can approach this same basic principle in another way if we now consider what I will call 'the atmosphere' in which our interview takes place. 'Atmosphere', used here in a special technical sense, is hard to define; but its creation or otherwise involves the way in which the interview is conducted; the degree of genuine understanding and concern; the relationship between helper and helped and so on. Or, to put it in another way, it is the feeling and impression, as seen by the client, of how far the particular counsellor is willing and able to understand, and to help over, the problem.

One of the most important ways in which we build up a good and positive 'atmosphere' is through our ability to listen to the client. Put in that way this sounds easy; and, if asked, most of us would claim to be 'good listeners'. In the sense in which we mean it here, however, listening is an active and skilled process, and one which makes considerable demands upon the listener. Moreover, in practice, surprisingly few of us are good listeners in this more specific form of this term.

If we are to be successful in this task, we must listen not only to what is said, but to how it is said. We must observe with care and skill the changes in voice tone, the gestures, the hesitations and the silences. We must learn to assess the feeling behind every comment or every silence. We must note what our client is unable to tell us, as well as what he is able to say. We must show our concern and our understanding by the way in which we listen. We must learn when to encourage, and how; and when not to press for information or comment which the teenager is not yet ready, or able, to bring out.

If we can, and in fact, do, listen in this way, two important and valuable benefits will result. Because we have listened, we shall have learnt what the problem *really* is; and, most important of all, what it means to the client. Secondly, by letting the adolescent 'talk out' his problem we shall have relieved him of some of his tension, and thereby have helped him to see his problem more clearly and as more capable of solution.

This process of constructive listening obviously must make very heavy demands, not only on the helper's patience, skill, understanding and genuine concern, but also upon his time. Indeed, it is sometimes claimed that this technique is too time-consuming to be practicable in the type of helping-situation which we are describing here. It is true, of course, that we cannot 'rush' this helping process, if we are to have any hope of success. But, whether we have five minutes or an hour for our interview, and whether it takes place in the relative peace of our office or at a chance meeting in the street, the client must be able to feel that this is genuinely his time with us, and his alone.

Sometimes, and indeed a great deal more often than we might expect, this ability to listen with genuine concern can be all the help that is needed to enable the teenager to 'solve his problem'. Obviously, however, there will be other instances where further help is needed. What form can this further help take?

Advice, guidance, support, discussion or a direct authoritarian comment on what should be done are all possible reactions on the helper's part at this point. Each of these forms of help can be appropriate and of value; but this will be true only if we remember, and make use of, certain very definite criteria in choosing which particular technique we should make use of on that particular occasion. For there is a very considerable risk that we will make our choice solely because we ourselves like, or want, to use that particular technique. But if we are to help the teenager under stress it is essential that we choose, and provide, that form of help which he or she needs at that particular time. It will require skilled and understanding judgment on our part; and a mature knowledge and recognition of our own prejudices and personal attitudes to achieve this necessary insight into what help our client really needs.

Moreover each of these various helping techniques has its own particular values and limitations. For example, unjustified reassurance, encouragement or praise which is unearned, unrealistic authoritarian demands, or impracticable advice will not be of value and, indeed, may well do actual harm.

These facts emphasize once again the value of constructive listening. After all, what other means could we use if we are to discover what the problem really is, or if we are to understand the teenager's real feelings about, and towards, his problem? And if we do not make this necessary preliminary 'diagnosis', how can we hope to choose the most appropriate form of 'treatment'?

It must not be supposed that the relatively simple techniques and concepts which I have described constitute the whole art of counselling. As I stated earlier, it would be impossible to cover so large and important a topic in one single lecture. Certainly it would be both wrong and dangerous to suggest that anyone should use full counselling methods without first having undergone adequate, and well-planned, selection and training for this task. Nevertheless, the teacher, the youth leader and others with similar responsibilities, can learn a great deal from an understanding of professional counselling skills. Moreover they can utilize, and adapt these methods in their equally important, but technically less complex, task of helping the teenager over his (or her) day-to-day problems. Such understanding will aid also the recognition of those cases where more skilled professional help is needed.

Whilst we must remember that much of our success in such a

helping role will depend on our own personal qualities, on our genuine concern to help and on our ability to recognize our own prejudices and limitations, we can, and should, refine the quality of our help by a study of human behaviour and motivation (both ours and that of the teenager) and by our ability to understand and use appropriately those special techniques and skills which stem from professional counselling.

Chapter VII

The Quality of Parenthood

Large annual conferences of this type[1] are a comparatively recent phenomenon; and a great deal of time, although surprisingly little research, has gone into the study of how to end such a conference. One favourite method is to select someone, and to ask him to sum up what has been said during the conference as a whole. This would be a difficult task in itself. But it is made more. difficult because the participants, who are obviously aware that the conference is coming to an end, view this fact with mixed feelings —sometimes with relief, but more frequently with regret. Half their concentration and thoughts are on which train they are going to catch home, on the sort of problems which are going to be on their desks, or in their clinics, when they get back there. One of the devastating events in any closing session is that a certain number of people always get up and walk out; and, although the speaker is intellectually aware that the legitimate reason for this is because they have to catch a train to Aberdeen or Penzance, the analogy of rats leaving a sinking ship is a very forceful piece of imagery for any speaker.

So, although I very greatly welcomed the privilege of being asked to speak today, and to close this annual conference, I felt that before I decided what to say, I should consider what the task of a closing speaker was. It seemed to me that, for this particular association, a very valid comparison was with the weaning process. After all, the young infant has a diet of milk, which contains all the necessary ingredients and which is easily digested; nor has he to make very much effort to imbibe his milk. In a way

[1] This lecture was delivered at the 1968 Annual Conference of the National Association for Maternal and Child Welfare.

a conference is rather like this. At a conference we are able to sit, comparatively free from our personal tensions, personal difficulties and the problems which we face in our jobs, and to listen to some very experienced and capable experts who give us the basic ingredients which—as in milk—have to some extent been predigested. All we have to do is to sit, and take it in. However, as the conference draws to a close, we realize that, enormously valuable as this basic diet has been, we now have to go home to our jobs and translate this wisdom into actual, complicated, individual crises, problems and situations. In other words, we have to do what the infant does at the point of weaning—begin to make rather more effort ourselves at imbibing and digesting. We can, and must, no longer rely purely on the basic principles. We have to face the reality of our work, just as the weaned child has to face the reality of coping with new and different types of food.

I see my task, therefore, as helping you over this weaning process. Obviously, in the very limited time available, I cannot give you a whole post-weaning diet. What I would like to do is to pick out one or two points which I think are significant in relation to this question of applying what we have learnt at this conference to our everyday tasks; and to focus this upon the basic conference theme of 'The Quality of Parenthood'.

In the early Celtic church there were two classes of saints. There were those who had been nominated and selected by Saint Patrick himself—these were, so to speak, Grade A saints—and there were those who had been selected by others. These were somewhat inferior. One of my favourite phantasies is to visualize the social situation when these two classes of saints—and worse still their wives—met! To return to reality, however, it seems to me that when professional people, administrators and so on, meet together, there often is a danger of our seeing ourselves as the grade A saints; and parents as the rather inferior, grade B, saints. There is a danger of our being too easily prepared to give a great deal of 'good' theoretical advice, much of which may be quite impracticable, and much of which may imply that parents do not try very hard, or are not very satisfactory people. Therefore, in talking to you about the quality of parenthood, I want to emphasize particularly the positive things about parents; and the ways in which we can help them in consequence.

In general terms, we can describe three types of parent. The great majority of parents are good, reasonably conscientious, and genuinely concerned about their children. Of course they make numerous mistakes; almost as many as you and I make professionally. Next, there are the parents who are unconcerned—a comparatively small group, but an important one. Finally there are those parents who are unable to cope for some reason or other. Let us consider briefly how you and I try to help these three different groups of parents.

The good, conscientious parent goes to PTA meetings, goes to the child welfare centre, reads the books, and acquires a great deal of good advice. Yet, when you come to think of it, how often does this advice provoke the very reaction which we want to avoid, namely a sense of failure? How often, in fact, do we consider of what the parent is *really* capable; or what the role of this particular parent is? Let me give you some very simple examples of this.

I am sure that one of the major advances in mental health in the post-war years has been the work of Bowlby and his associates on maternal deprivation. Very few people would quarrel with the importance of this. However, because this concept has been so much over-sold, we quite frequently see parents who become anxious and really guilty if, quite legitimately, they have to be separated from their child for a few hours, or for a day. We see parents who become extremely guilty when, again for legitimate reasons, they may not be able to visit their child every day in hospital. Surely we have to achieve a balance here. Are these children going to be more disturbed and distressed by a brief period of separation; or by the guilt, anxiety and lack of confidence which the parents will build up over this?

It is often said that one should not frustrate children; but how does one avoid frustrating children? Frustration is a necessary experience; it is part of the process of development. We make pious remarks about 'mother love', and about loving one's child; but how often do we remember to add that genuine love, genuine concern, involves the ability to say 'no' as well as to say 'yes'? How often do we remember that love involves the capacity to be cross as well as to be pleased as each is relevant? Genuine love and genuine concern for one's child also involve the need to withhold when necessary, as well as to give. In other words, how often do we produce, by our good advice, a demand on the parents which is not only impossible of achievement, but which must make parents guilty and unsure?

I saw a mother the other day who said to me, in quite genuine distress, 'I've been to see the school dentist and he says that my children ought to eat an apple after each meal every day.' That was good, sound, dental advice; but this mother had six children and a comparatively small income, and she was very genuinely worried because she could not afford to follow this advice. Do we, with good parents, think often enough about building up their confidence; or about the positive ways of helping them to realize the things which they *can* cope with? Or are we more concerned to give dogmatic, theoretical advice, and thereby provoke the very thing we want to avoid? How often do we forget that, as professional people, *we* are intellectually concerned with the problems of child development and child rearing? We are not emotionally involved, whereas the parent *is* emotionally involved but not so concerned with the theoretical aspects. We have to learn how to translate our very sound professional, technical and theoretical knowledge into something which will be emotionally meaningful to the parent.

Let us move on to the next group. I do not want to deal at any length with the uninterested parent, the parent who could not care less, the parent who does not bother, since this group is rather outside our present field. The only comment I would make here is that, in the area of juvenile delinquency for example where we find the highest proportion—although it is still not a very great proportion—of parents of this type, we can see a very interesting example of our thinking, in that, in the one area where it would be particularly valuable to bring in statutory control and action at an early age to remedy the problem, modern legislation tends to make such action even more difficult to achieve.

However, I would like to talk at rather greater length about the parent who is unable to cope, the parent under stress. Several types of parent in this category have been described in the papers read at this conference. I want to pick up just one or two points about them.

First of all there is the parent who is unable to cope for the reasons which I have given already, for example the parent who fears that to seek advice is to make a confession of failure or the parent who feels that help should not be necessary, or the good parent, indeed the ultra-conscientious parent, who puts his head in the sand rather than face up to a difficult situation.

On the whole handicapped parents, psychotic parents and so on cope remarkably well. But how often do we realize what an immense burden normal child-rearing can be for them? In my own speciality it is generally accepted that, from the point of view of the adult patient, it is very sound therapeutic policy to have as short a period of hospitalization as possible before returning the patient to the community. However, I feel sure that many hospital psychiatrists do not realize the enormous burden which the 'recovered', but chronic psychotic patient can represent to the family. As a child psychiatrist I see, for example, the schizophrenic mother who is capable of being back in the community, but who at the same time is quite incapable of providing any spontaneous emotional feeling for her child. Such a child may suffer as severely from deprivation as if the mother were not there. This is an area where we have to stress that, if the patient's need is to be out of hospital, then we must do a very great deal more to help to support the family and in particular the child.

Then there are those parents who are able to cope in the ordinary way, but who may be faced with special difficulties or stresses. This morning we heard a very masterly description of the problems of the parents of handicapped children. How much do you and I, professionally or administratively, do to help here? When an accurate assessment has been made, do we always spend time describing this to parents, discussing it and explaining it to them; and helping them to accept emotionally, not only the limitations of the child—which is vital—but also the possibilities? How often do we realize how intensely guilty the parents of a handicapped child may feel? Such guilt may prevent them from facing up to the child's disability; and they go from hospital to hospital to find out if something more can be done. Alternatively, they may see the child as a hopeless disaster for whom nothing can be done. How often are we honest with the parents and capable of seeing their emotional involvement?

I saw a girl a week or two ago who had a paralysed right arm. Her parents were both professional people—both doctors, in fact, but because of their intense feeling of guilt and failure this young adolescent girl had never really been 'allowed' in any way to be handicapped. Her parents had desperately taken her around to all and sundry, and given her all sorts of exercises and so on, in an attempt to get her to use her weak, damaged, right arm. The emphasis had always been on 'you are normal', with an implied criticism towards her and her handicap. Her mother said to me in the course of the initial interview, 'I could not bear to think of my daughter as being anything but perfect.' The girl was referred to me because as a young adolescent she was being difficult and sulky, and very nearly delinquent. We did not get very far in the early stages of our interview until I said to her, 'When you came in to see me, what did you expect me to say?' She looked at me sulkily, and replied resentfully, 'I supposed you were going to tell me, like everybody else has told me, to use my right arm properly.' I replied, 'No. As a matter of fact, what I have been thinking ever since you came into the room, ever since I watched you take your coat and gloves off, was how skilfully you were using your left arm to substitute for the right.' She suddenly stopped sulking, and then she said, 'No one has ever said that to me before.' I am not suggesting that this was a magical point which produced a 'cure'; but here at least was a positive starting-point. Someone was prepared to say to this girl, and to her parents: 'Look, this is what this girl can do. This is what this girl cannot do.'

Yet another point must be raised here. We must remember, too, that the handicapped child can be difficult; the handicapped child can play up; the handicapped child can be naughty; the handicapped child will often try to sidestep what he can do but does not want to do. How far do we help parents to put pressure on the handicapped child? How hard is it, for instance, for the parents of a blind child to let him take certain risks so that he can discover what he can do? Is it not asking a great deal of the parents of a handicapped child; is it not asking a great deal of the community whose members tend to be—as the previous speaker said—themselves emotionally involved in this problem; is it not asking a great deal of all these people to be able to put this pressure on, to be able to be cross with a handicapped child when necessary, to say 'no' as well as 'yes', to encourage as well as to discourage? All these are things with which you and I professionally can help. The parent who feels unable to cope can often be helped to do just this.

Many of these factors apply to the other parental groups which have been mentioned in this conference—the parents with adopted children and foster parents for example. How careful are children's departments in assessing what sort of child can be fostered? Do they always remember that every normal, good, foster-parent is going to need—if she is going to be successful—some 'feedback' from the child, some sort of emotional response? Yet one sees children who would have coped much better in the emotionally less demanding atmosphere of a small children's home than with foster parents; and who fail in the foster-situation—sometimes only to be re-fostered yet again! Have we given more thought to the possibilities of fostering than to its limitations? Further, just as I have commented about the handicapped child and his parents, how honest are we with foster parents? How much do we positively help them with the difficulties of their task?

This brings me to the central theme which lies behind the whole of this conference—the sort of supportive help which we *can* give. One of your speakers said how nice it could be not just to cope with the 'crisis' itself but to give supportive help throughout the whole child-rearing period, so that the parents could see the growth and development of the child as a smooth, satisfactory process, and not just as a series of difficulties. Our problem is that, in reality, a great deal of child-rearing is a series of difficulties!

I agree that one has to provide support, and be available, to the parent throughout the whole child-rearing period. Nevertheless, the point at which we will make our maximum impact, the point where most often we will make our first real contact, is the point of 'crisis'. Let me give you another example from recent clinical experience. About nine months ago we had referred to the clinic a very difficult thirteen-year-old girl who was highly dramatic, a skilful actress, a manipulator, very much at risk, and a complete nuisance to everybody. She was referred by the school because of a great deal of showing off and dramatic behaviour there. Her parents were a pleasant middle-class couple, very genuinely fond of and concerned about their daughter, but quite unable to face up to the fact that she was difficult. They said of the school situation, 'Of course, you know, these things happen in schools. This is the way girls behave.' They were not, at this stage, able to accept that there was a problem and therefore they were not really able to accept the need for help. They agreed to my seeing the girl from time to time, and I did so. They were not unco-operative or difficult parents; they were parents who found themselves unable to face up to a situation. We continued to maintain this superficial contact, until very recently the mother rang me up in a state of great alarm to say, 'You were perfectly right. Something disastrous has happened. Could you come and see us?' We arranged an urgent interview, and I saw the mother and the girl. What had happened was in line with her customary pattern. As an act of sheer dramatic bravado she had stayed out all night, and having stayed out she had to tell the police a fictitious story to account for this. The resulting complications were inevitable and considerable. At this point of 'crisis' parents and girl were accessible; they were able to accept the need for help.

What does one do at this stage? Does one just say, 'I told you so'? or, 'If only you had let me do some preventive work this would not have happened'? Or does one make use of the basic relationship achieved at a quite superficial level during the quiescent period and build upon it by helping in, and over, the crisis situation? Clearly the last alternative is the right one. Moreover sometimes one cannot even begin to provide supportive help until there is a crisis. As a quite different sort of example of this, I recently read an article on the surgical treatment of ulcerative colitis in which the writer stated that the correct treatment was surgical, and that operative surgery was best carried out during the quiescent period between attacks. The writer went on to say how extremely difficult it was to get any patient, during this quiescent period when he is perfectly well, to see the necessity for active surgery.

Accordingly we must provide the supportive services and have these ready both to make an initial contact and to come in at the essential point of crisis when people become more accessible, when in fact the unwilling client so often becomes willing to accept help.

I would like to finish with a comment on one other important theme of this conference—the problem of inter-professional co-operation. This point was mentioned this morning; and it has been stressed in many of the other papers. Co-operation between the various agencies, the various authorities, the various professional workers, is the one essential need if we are to succeed in our task. We have to learn how to work together. I recently heard a very eminent educational administrator say at a meeting, 'We believe in co-ordination in my area. What we do is to send copies of everything to everybody.' But this is not, in my view, working together. There is a common and dangerous tendency for all the professions (including my own) to regard other professional workers, and other agencies, as somehow inferior. Too often we feel that to transfer a child, a parent or a family to another agency is a confession of our own 'failure'. Surely what we have to do, if we are to achieve genuine co-operation, is to recognize our own limitations, as well as our own skills. We must learn to appreciate what we can do and what we cannot do; and equally what other agencies can do better than we can, and what they cannot do. We have to make personal contact with other people in the field; to know a great deal about the other social services as well as our own. We must be able, perhaps above all, to trust each other.

Since this question of co-operation is my final theme, let me end with a quotation which I have used on a good many other occasions, and which I think illustrates, if in crude Elizabethan terms, what co-operation really means. For there is a quotation from an Elizabethan dramatist which sums it all up:

'To be bedded with someone with whom you are at ease is to be truly bedded; but to be bedded with someone with whom you are at unease, why truly t'were better not to go to bed.'

Chapter VIII

Evaluation with a View to Action (The Diagnostic Role of the Child Guidance Clinic Team)

We are very aware of the privilege and responsibility it is, as a clinic team, to be asked to provide the basic material for an NAMH inter-clinic conference, particularly as we are the first provincial clinic to be asked to do so in the present series. I would emphasize one point from the beginning—that although I take full responsibility for the shortcomings or otherwise of this lecture, the thinking which lies behind it owes a great deal to all my colleagues in the clinic team.

As with all NAMH inter-clinic conferences, much of the important work will be achieved in the subsequent group-discussions. Consequently my own function in this lecture will be an attempt to consider and redefine our own thinking about those problems with which any team is daily in contact at every child guidance clinic. I have assumed, therefore, that the purpose of this basic material is to provide a focus for discussion; or, to change the analogy, to create a framework within which we all can think out, and discuss, our own ideas and experiences. I hope to give you some idea of the techniques of evaluation which are used in one individual, large and quite busy clinic; techniques which have been built up over a number of years by a team, whose members have come from a variety of backgrounds and training sources. I do not mean to suggest that this is an ideal evaluation technique which all clinics should adopt. It may not even be an ideal method for our own clinic. Indeed, in the course of our clinic team seminars on this basic material, fraught as they were with some anxiety and tension on occasions, we have already learnt a good deal about our own methods. The purpose in presenting this material and information is that others can compare and contrast it with their own methods, in an attempt to see whether there are any basic principles and ideas which we could all learn from each other. Those of us who have had the experience of working in, or with, a number of clinics are only too well aware of the very great differences of techniques and standards which exist as between various clinics. In discussion we often tend to accentuate these difficulties and differences. But what I personally feel to be our primary task is to determine those basic principles which we could all accept as 'good child guidance practice'. Unless first we hold certain accepted basic principles in common, it is inevitable that those detailed variations which also exist can be both dangerous and disruptive to our work in the child guidance service.

It is obvious that, in the time available, I can only describe certain specific items of our evaluation technique. Inevitably my comments may appear to be both rather dogmatic and over-simplified. Moreover, I have had to describe our evaluation procedure as a series of separate events and entities, although in practice, of course, these separate 'compartments' are not divided in such a neat and water-tight manner.

The first item with which I would like to deal, although very briefly, is the significance of the referral documents. In our clinic, there are, as a rule, the referral letter and a preliminary written report obtained from the child's school. Normally we avoid contacting the referral agency at this stage, because we do not wish to obtain *too* much information before our own diagnostic interview. It is of course a matter for discussion whether this is a sound policy or not. We feel that pre-referral information can attract too much attention too early; and focus it in the wrong direction. Yet nevertheless we believe that the referral documents do have two valuable functions. First, these will often indicate the emotional climate in which the referral has taken place, and thereby be of considerable potential evaluation significance.

Secondly, we find that the presenting symptom, as described in the referral documents, is often very different from the presenting symptom as described by the parent at the beginning of the first interview, or as it appears subsequently. Again, these differences may be quite significant. If the clinic is a community agency which works in close contact with other agencies in the area, it may gain a shrewd suspicion of the real nature of the problem from the referral documents alone. For example, we already had learnt a good deal about the problem, when we received, as we did recently, a referral letter about a three-and-a-half-year-old child who was biting other children, which said: 'I refer him to the child guidance clinic but I would much sooner have sent him to the dentist to have his teeth out'!

We must now consider two other, and more important, aspects of the evaluation technique: namely the role of the educational psychologist, and the role of the psychiatric social worker. But first I must describe some relevant aspects of our own administrative procedures. In our clinic, we aim to make the interval between the referral and the initial interview as brief as possible; it is usually only a matter of a few weeks, and in an urgent case it may only be a day or two. Do not think that we have no waiting list, but we feel it better that any necessary waiting period should occur between those initial interviews and the subsequent assessment interview by the child psychiatrist. In our clinic, therefore, the educational psychologist and the psychiatric social worker see the problem whilst it is still very 'hot'.

Secondly, the child and the parents (we invite both parents; and surprisingly often both come) attend the clinic together. The child is seen by the psychologist at the same time as the psychiatric social worker is interviewing the parents. This again is a point worthy of discussion. Yet the very fact that the parents' and child's first experience of the clinic is in coming to it together is something quite important in itself. But we have to realize too that, as opposed to other methods of initial contact, this technique will produce its own variations in response, and thereby colour the evaluation, as well as the therapeutic situation. Similarly the policy of seeing the parents at the clinic, as opposed to during a home visit, will produce differences of reaction; and, if we are not alert to the differing impact of such a procedure we can easily underestimate the parent's strengths, if only because the mother seems perhaps so much more under strain in the clinic than she might be if she had been seen in her own home. It is in the light of these individual variations of technique that we must now consider the role of each of the members of the clinic team.

The educational psychologist has quite a number of inter-related functions, some of which would be generally accepted, but some of which might be more open to dispute and discussion. First, but not necessarily foremost, he has to estimate the child's intelligence level. Clearly, much skill and experience will go into the choice of the most appropriate test in each individual case. But, in general terms, our choice would be for the WISC test as giving a wider and more detailed breakdown of both the child's potential and reactions. Secondly, in many instances the psychologist will need to estimate the child's attainments level. We do not do this as an automatic routine, but it is done where we have reason to suppose that it is especially important and significant.

Nor do we use projection tests as a routine. Our view would be—and again I think this is a matter for discussion—that projection tests which illustrate family relationship patterns are valuable; but we are not so happy about the use with children of those projection tests which are intended to illuminate personality patterns.

But it is obvious that the educational psychologist has a great deal more to do than only to obtain an intelligence level assessment. He has to note the child's reaction to a structured and set intellectual task—which after all is what the test is to the child. The degree of concentration, the rapidity of response and so on, all may be significant, not only in assessing the actual scoring, but in assessing also the child's reaction to similar problems in his school environment. The intelligence test may be emotionally very significant to some children, for example to the child who is aware that he has come to the clinic because everybody has said that he is backward. Often the educational psychologist may have to decide if the child is anxious because he is backward, or if he is backward because he is anxious? Most psychologists would seem to agree that the child's reaction to certain items in the various tests may indicate the possibility of emotional disturbance. Our own comment on this point, and only after a good deal of discussion, suggests that some items (for instance, the 'plan of search') can be of value as pointers, but only as pointers.

There remains another aspect of the educational psychologist's interview which requires our consideration. I do not myself believe that any psychologist could obtain an accurate and full assessment of a child in an entirely sterile, emotionally neutral, atmosphere. I am sure that for success some sort of relationship must exist between the psychologist and the child. Moreover the psychologist, particularly when he is seeing the case at so very acute a stage, almost inevitably will come up against such factors as the child's attitude towards coming to the clinic, and towards the presenting problem and so on. Normally that part of the educational psychologist's test interview which deals with actual testing is a very structured affair, in which he has in effect to say to the child, 'We will do so and so.' In our own clinic, therefore, the educational psychologist will have a period in addition with the child which is much more in the nature of an 'interview' than a test situation. In this 'interview', the psychologist can talk to the child about his interests; ask him in neutrally phrased questions about his home, or school; ask about and, even discuss, the reason (as the child sees it) for his referral to the clinic, if these seem to be significant in the particular case. In other words, the educational psychologist should be free to discuss with the child certain aspects of the emotional problem. Now we are very well aware that this may have potential dangers, and that this policy would not be universally approved. But before it is prematurely condemned it is justifiable to stress a number of important points.

It must be remembered that, in our own clinic, the educational psychologist is seeing the case very soon after the referral. There may then follow a rather longer interval before the child psychiatrist sees the child; and the length of that interval will be determined by the degree of urgency as assessed at the initial interviews. To be able to evaluate these emotional factors demands of the educational psychologist certain special interests and special experience, in addition to his basic skills as a psychologist. He must be able to handle whatever emotional material comes out. He must be aware of the significance of that material, and take care not to go too deeply into the problem at that stage. Inevitably, the fact that these points are taken up by the psychologist in his initial interview must colour the child psychiatrist's subsequent interviews with the child. The psychiatrist must know in detail therefore what has happened in that first interview; since otherwise his own evaluation may be thrown off balance. With these provisos, my own impression—and I am speaking here personally as the psychiatrist who would get the 'kick' if there was one—is that this preliminary working out of the secondary reactive layer of anxiety, the anxiety about coming to the clinic for example, is often a useful step towards making the subsequent interviews more valuable and effective. But this is a point which is debatable.

Let us turn next to the role of the psychiatric social worker. As I have said, she sees the parents at the first visit, whilst the educational psychologist is seeing the child. This immediately introduces one situation which is worth observing. For in such a situation both mother and child have to suffer a 'separation' from each other in the clinic. The reaction of each to this separation can be informative.

In the psychiatric social worker's actual role with the parent, her initial interview, by tradition, is built around the taking of a social history. A point which I would like to raise here is whether the taking of this history is *the* important task, or whether what actually happens at the interview is the essential factor. Moreover this is a very material question for discussion, not only by the psychiatric social workers themselves but also by the other members of the team. I am sure that there are many members of other disciplines who regard the psychiatric social worker as 'falling down' on her job unless she provides a nice accurate factual history, including all the details as to when the child cut his first teeth and so on. But is this in fact her total task? Or could it be done better? After all, this interview between parent and psychiatric social worker is probably a very new experience for the parent. A parent might find it difficult to understand, or to accept, an interview which did not consist to some extent of history taking, and to some extent of question and answer. Obviously, too, we do need some historical information if we are fully to understand the present dynamic situation itself. To give one example, the historical development material is important for our understanding of the present relationship between parent and child.

What I would stress here, however, is that there is all the difference in the world between obtaining what is purely a factual history, and obtaining a history which indicates attitudes towards the various historical events in the child's life. For instance, it is not just a question of what the parent is able, or unable, to say. The way in which it is said, together with all those subtle nuances of the interview, are vitally important.

There are certain special areas, of course, in which we need particular information. We need to know, in detail, about the parents' attitude during those crucial developmental phases—phases such as the onset of aggressive behaviour, the stage of growing independence in the child, weaning, sleeping problems, feeding problems and the like; but we need this 'history' not so much as factual detail, but in terms of what these situations, these experiences meant to the parents and to the child. We need to know details also of the more recent, more immediate, historical material; and of the nature of the presenting symptoms. Again the importance lies not only in the presenting symptom as it was first given by the parents, but in the *real* presenting symptom as it appears in the course of the interview; the real difficulty, the real problem, the real anxiety as the parent sees it. We need to know how the parent feels about coming to the clinic. What does it mean for her? What does the presenting difficulty mean for her? These are points which may often be discovered, at least initially, by question and answer. But not by question and answer alone, or in a purely factual sense. Equally we need to know something about the relationship pattern within the family, about the sibling rivalries, about relationships between parent and child. All those things are part of history-taking in the sense in which we mean it. By tradition, the psychiatric social worker also asks a good deal about the mother and father's own history. But here again there is a clear distinction between a factual history and what is probably the real point—what has that life experience meant to them in terms of the presenting problem? How far, and in what way, do they identify the child with some 'bad' or 'good' figure in their own environmental patterns, or in their own life history? Does their own personal history make them especially vulnerable to their child's own problem?

There remains one further facet of the psychiatric social worker's interview which is immensely important, namely her assessment of the parent as a person. This assessment must be made not only in terms of the parent's flexibility or potential insight, not only in terms of her strengths or maturity, but also in terms of the parent's relationship with the psychiatric social worker, used as an illustration of her relationships and potential for relationships, in other directions. I would stress again the essential importance of this aspect of the interview. It will be obvious, therefore, that in an interview of this sort the psychiatric social worker has to make many very difficult technical decisions. When should she ask questions? When should she press, or not press, for information? There may be instances when to ask a question will be to force the parent to bring out material which she is not yet ready to produce. Equally well, there will be other instances when the parent greatly needs to bring out material, but cannot manage to do so, at that particular point, without some help. To sum up the pattern of the social history interview as I see it, it must be a very flexible process; structured in the sense that it has a certain function, a certain purpose and a certain professional discipline, but flexible enough to include not only what the psychiatric social worker thinks is necessary (and not always what the clinic thinks is necessary), but also the needs of the parent in that particular interview setting. The psychiatric social worker must be very sensitive to those needs, and to the leads that the client gives her.

In our clinic, the psychiatric social worker and the educational psychologist make their initial evaluation at the end of these first two interviews. How far are such evaluations valid at that point? We have to remember that each will make an assessment and judgment only of what has happened in his or her particular interview to date. Their aim is not to evaluate the whole situation, the whole diagnostic picture. Rather is it an attempt to say: this is what happened at my interview; this is what I think the significance is, so far. Within such a framework their assessments at this stage are very much worth while.

In passing, I would like to mention briefly one other point which arose during the team seminars and which seems relevant here. How far does this special interview technique give any more information than would be obtained by an intelligent, capable layman interviewing the parent? We are confident that, in their interviews, the psychiatric social worker, the child psychiatrist and the educational psychologist are using certain professional skills as a valid measuring tool; and that each obtains from the interview a very great deal more than would be obtained by anyone without such professional skills. In the first place, the interviewer is using learned professional techniques, based on experience, training and technical knowledge; next, he is a competent and skilled observer of the indirect as well as the more obvious aspects of the interviews. Finally he is aware of, and has insight into, his own personal prejudices and attitudes.

I would like now to consider the role of the child psychiatrist in the task of evaluation. In our clinic the psychiatrist's interview differs in a number of important ways from the interviews which have gone before. First there has been a considerable interval of time since the referral. This fact, plus the nature of the original interviews, means that the secondary anxiety has often settled; and the presenting symptom itself may even have decreased or disappeared. (I do not mean of course that there has been a 'cure'; but nevertheless the pattern of the psychiatrist's interview will be altered by these factors.)

Then for the first time the two streams of material from the educational psychologist and psychiatric social worker will have come together as basic material for a third interview. The psychiatrist thereby will be much more aware of the detailed nature of the problem. Thus, whilst his interview can be much more flexible, and much less structured, it can also be given a much more specific focus and aim.

What does the child psychiatrist try to do in his interview?—and it may be quite revealing that our own clinic staff were very determined to know just what the psychiatrist *did* do! In his interview with the child, his first task is to observe the child as a physical entity; that is to say, the child's physical build, his overt signs of tension, his gait, his movements and so on. Secondly he has to assess the child in certain situations which are an inevitable part of the interview, e.g. in the separation which occurs from the parent when he collects the child, in the child's reaction to the interview itself, in the child's choice of play material and so on.

The 'freer' nature of the interview may give a very different picture from that obtained from the more structured, more controlled, interview by the psychologist. The psychiatrist must remember this point when he comes to assess the nature, and the content, of the child's spontaneous activity, drawing and painting, including their absence or presence, and their pattern and significance. In our own procedure we do not discuss with the child the content of his activity at the diagnostic interview unless there are special reasons for doing so. But of course the child spontaneously will often produce comments about his own activity.

Next—and this again is a point worthy of discussion—I feel that the child psychiatrist should assess the child's reaction to certain specific situations, and to certain specific topics, which can be put into the interview in any desired order (or omitted if this seems wiser). For example, it would seem valuable at this initial interview to ask the child, in a neutrally phrased way, questions such as 'Who lives at home?' or 'How do you feel about school?' The purpose of these questions is not to produce factually accurate information, but to indicate attitudes in the child.

Finally, the child psychiatrist has to form an assessment of the child's relationship with him; again as an illustration of the child's potential for, and experience of, other human relationships. To succeed in this the psychiatrist must be sensitive to the influence of his own attitude, and of his own encouragement (or otherwise) to the child.

The child psychiatrist has another important role. In our clinic, at this stage, he sees the parents. (Once again we normally invite both parents; and surprisingly often both come.) I personally regard this as one of the most difficult interviews with which the psychiatrist is normally called upon to deal. For his function here is in many ways anomalous. He is cutting across what is to become a whole series of subsequent interviews between psychiatric social worker and parent. He is in the position of having to form an evaluation; and then of explaining to the parents the nature of the problem, and the help which the clinic can or cannot give. It has been said that this is a breach of the team method, in that the psychiatrist is taking upon himself here that authoritarian role of which he is said to be traditionally so fond. I would stress that, in the evaluation which he makes at this stage, as well as in what he says to the parents, he is using the material from the team sources of psychiatric social worker and educational psychologist's diagnostic interviews, as well as from his own interview. It is essential that the psychiatrist should remember that his is only one of a series of interviews with the parent; and that he must be able, and willing, to 'hand back' the interview relationship to the psychiatric social worker. Moreover, the psychiatrist's interview with the parents can sometimes provide important new evaluation material. With the interval that has elapsed since she saw the psychiatric social worker, the parent may be able to bring out more (or less) material; or she may bring out that material in a different way. The psychiatrist having no need for fact finding at this particular stage of his interview is free to allow much more to come out spontaneously. Finally, the parent's reaction to the psychiatrist's discussion of the problem, and the possible clinic help, is often of very great significance. This illustrates a point of considerable importance, namely that we can never define exactly where evaluation ends and where therapy begins.

Having briefly, and rather dogmatically, described some aspects of the role of the various team members, I must now say something about the techniques of interdisciplinary communication. Can these be improved? What more can we do to make sure that each member of the team does contribute fully to the evaluation process? There are, I think, three ways in which this can be done, and we have used all three methods in our own clinic. First, there is the full-scale, and traditional, case conference, in which every member of the clinic staff participates, the team members who have been responsible for the particular case presenting the material for general discussion. We would like to have a regular case conference once a week. We are fully aware of the very great value of this type of full case conference, which is a learning process for every member of the team no matter how experienced; and a teaching process of great importance to students or other professional visitors to the clinic. But it is extremely time-consuming; and therefore it is practicable to discuss only a small proportion of one's new cases in full case conference. We must therefore consider a second, and alternative, method: the rather less formal discussion of the case as between the three members of the team who have handled it up to that point. This method has some obvious advantages. It takes much less time, in that it is not necessary to produce the whole of the case material in detail since this information is already known to the three team-members involved. But this technique also presents some reality difficulties. In our own clinic, I, as only one of the three child psychiatrists, may be concerned with cases with any permutation and combination of four psychiatric social workers and three educational psychologists. Clearly this would demand a very large number of discussions with different people every week, to say nothing of the fact that cases under treatment will also require discussion between team members. This must represent a very real problem in any clinic which is working under pressure—as most clinics do! We have to decide, therefore, whether team discussion is essential, and something which *must* have preference. Because we are so wedded to the team method, do we tend to assume that, without discussion, the team process will fall to the ground?

There is a third method of 'discussion' into which we are often forced by sheer pressure of time. We can read each other's notes—and I really mean read these, because in some clinics nobody ever dreams of reading anybody else's notes—they merely look at the headings. But if we read our colleague's notes with understanding, and if we know these colleagues well, then we can obtain much valuable information in this way, thus leaving only certain special points to be discussed verbally. I do not suggest this is an ideal method; but it is an attempt to find a method which is practicable within the reality situation of the clinic's total task.

However, the techniques of inter-professional communication raise issues which could take up a whole conference—and indeed perhaps should take up a whole conference one day. There is certainly a need to give serious thought to our methods of recording notes, and to our use of technical 'jargon'. For example, in notes written for oneself, one might use a very simple word like 'inadequate'. I would do so because this word conjures up for me a total picture of a sort of situation, a sort of child, a sort of reaction pattern. In other words, 'inadequate', used in this way, brings to my mind many points far beyond the narrow dictionary, or even the technical, definition of that word. Yet to someone else, who is equally technically knowledgeable, it may mean something quite different.

In the short time that is left, I would like to discuss what is really the central point about evaluation, namely: what is its aim and purpose? I was interested to note that in the title of this Conference, the word 'evaluation' was used rather than 'diagnosis'. I am sure that this phrase 'evaluation with a view to action' does give a more genuine and meaningful description of what we try to do. It does not suggest that we are concerned only to provide a 'diagnostic label'. Now I am aware that many people prefer to have such a neat diagnostic label. But my own feeling is that, if one concentrates too much, or only, on providing the 'diagnostic label', one can lose sight of the total situation and of the real needs of the child and his family. After all, if one's sole aim is to design a 'diagnostic label', one will strive so hard to find out all the factual details too early. As a result one may come to ignore entirely the emotional significance of these details to the client.

As I see it, the purpose of evaluation is to form an assessment of the child—the total child in his total environment—to assess what potential strengths there are in that setting; to assess what are the stresses and strains in the situation, and how far it will be possible to modify these stresses. In other words, our task of evaluation must be directed much more to the needs of the child and his family, than to the needs of the clinic (who may find a neat diagnostic label convenient) or of the administrative authority (who may demand full statistical tables at the end of each year).

This is a point of fundamental importance, since, if we are to evaluate in this broader sense, the whole pattern and technique of the process must be geared to that aim. Only in such circumstances can evaluation and treatment go hand in hand.

Finally, in making our evaluation with a view to action, we must devise not only a theoretically ideal programme of action—in other words what we would think *ought* to be done in this case. We must also remember, and consider, what *can* be done in this particular case, within the framework, within the difficulties and the limitations of our own clinic; its staffing, its experience, its case-load and so on. We must face up always to the reality situation. We must decide what can be done in our particular clinic, and what cannot be done.

This double evaluation is of great importance; but it does not mean that we should sit down complacently under our clinic's limitations and make no further effort. Many of us (defensively) find ourselves thinking that, because we are short-handed, we can do no therapy at all. But if we strike a balance between what we can do in our own particular reality setting, and what we would regard as good child guidance—or even ideal child guidance practice; and if we do this with real insight into the problem, we can put good quality even into our own limited resources. For, unless we are to see our difficulties, and our considerable differences of techniques, in terms of sound basic concepts, and good basic child guidance method, we cannot hope to make any real progress in our task.

Chapter IX

Relationship Therapy and Casework

A psychiatrist, invited to talk on a casework topic to an audience of skilled and experienced caseworkers, approaches the task with diffidence; and with something of the apprehension of Daniel entering the den of lions. However, I am made easier by the thought that much of what I know about casework has been gained from the quite considerable number of psychiatric social workers with whom I have worked in some twenty years of professional life.

It is always wise to define one's terms; but it is especially important to do so here. For two viewpoints, and as I hope to show mistaken viewpoints, are frequently expressed when this topic is under discussion. To many analysts, theirs is the only real form of psychotherapy; and they see a vast increase in the number of trained analysts as the only possible solution to the nation's need for adequate psychotherapeutic facilities. Of course, I am not attempting to decry the significance and value of psychoanalysis as a treatment technique, or as a research tool, or as the basis of other forms of psychotherapy. But it remains true that of the general (as opposed to the selected) client population, only a comparatively small number will have the capacity, or potential, for a full analytical approach. For very many, a less intensive form of therapy would be the method of choice, even in the unlikely event of the facilities for analysis becoming unlimited. Equally, for many psychiatric social workers, the term casework has come to mean only an intensive interpretive technique. How often does the phrase 'this client appears unsuitable for casework' when used by the psychiatric social worker in her assessment of her client, really mean 'unsuitable for intensive casework'? Has a tendency grown up to regard the less intensive forms of therapy and casework as somehow inferior; and, with it, a danger that the intensity of the therapy attempted will be governed more by the training level—and dare we say the professional ambitions—of the therapist or caseworker, than by the level of therapy which is most appropriate to the client's needs and capacity? Surely each level of therapy has its place; and thus each can be of equal value in its appropriate place.

There is a similar tendency to regard casework as the 'poor relation' of psychotherapy. This is a serious error, for again each in its appropriate case will be the method of choice, and with the appropriate client each is of equal value. Most of the comparisons made between psychotherapy and casework seem to be based on differences of technique, on the varying use of the transference, the 'depth' of the treatment, and so on. Yet these differences are valid only if we contrast casework with psychoanalysis itself. Excluding this specialized technique I suggest that in principle the basic techniques are similar, and that the only valid distinctions between psychotherapy and casework lie in differences of setting and in the different expectations of the client. These distinctions can be well illustrated in another field. Balint(1) points out how greatly the psychotherapeutic technique of the family doctor will be influenced by the setting in which he works. His contact will be with the family as a whole and not just with the individual patient, and the duration of his contact will not be governed by psychotherapeutic factors alone. He will need to help the patient over other difficulties also, physical illness, child-birth, material problems and the like. Balint shows clearly how, in such a setting, the practitioner can successfully use modifications of psychotherapeutic techniques which would be impossible for the psychotherapist in the isolation of his consulting room; yet the fundamental concepts on which these two methods are based are the same for both. A similar relationship is true as between psychotherapy and casework. Although he must become aware of the influence of environmental factors, the therapist is concerned with his patient very much as an individual person within the setting of his consulting room. In therapy he will not wish to involve himself greatly with that environmental pattern, with the other members of the patient's family, or with the reality situation. By tradition the patient comes to him with this same expectation, to be 'treated' for his 'illness'. The client's expectation from the caseworker will be subtly, but importantly, different. He will expect rather to have his 'problem solved', and be less ready to see himself as involved in treatment. In her turn, the caseworker, no matter how zealously she wishes to guard the person-to-person relationship, will almost certainly find herself concerned to some extent (and sometimes to a major degree) with the environmental milieu of the client, and with the people and events in that milieu. If, therefore, I now use the words 'therapy' and 'casework' as interchangeable, it is with a realization of these differences of setting and expectation; but with the emphasis on the basic similarities of principle and technique which unite them; and which make both equal, and each the method of choice in its appropriate setting and individual case.

It would be agreed by all of us that an inter-personal relationship lies behind any form of successful therapy or indeed behind any attempt to help another human being in difficulty or distress. What then do I mean by the term 'relationship therapy'? Put in its simplest terms, it differs from more intensive forms of psychotherapy and casework in the way in which the client initially and consciously visualizes the worker's function.

To extend and refine this elementary definition it is necessary to study in some detail two aspects of the situation—the assessment of and the criteria for the client's suitability for relationship therapy, and the differences of technique between this and the more intensive forms of treatment.

In making our assessment for relationship therapy we use three methods, all three are legitimate casework tools; all three are closely interrelated. Two are obvious and need only be mentioned: the historical record of the client's opportunities for, and his use and experience of, human relationships from his earlier fundamental parental relationships to the present day; and in his capacity for a relationship in the here-and-now situation of our own preliminary interviews with him. The third aspect of our problem has been perhaps rather less fully studied: the assessment of our own role and part in this relationship. What sort of relationship does this client need at this stage, and how far can, or should, we provide it? It is in this sector of the assessment that we draw most on our knowledge of psychological theory, and on our experience in analysis, or in intensive casework. It is here too that we need most of all good casework and psychiatric consultation facilities. For, as I hope to show you, we may have to assume roles that are more difficult for us personally to sustain than the more 'passive' role we adopt in intensive therapy.

At first sight, the criteria of suitability for relationship therapy appears more like a list of contra-indications for intensive treatment. Yet they should not be considered only in this negative way; for they are also pointers towards a constructive and legitimate form of casework.

The first criterion is a limited degree of conscious desire for help and especially for change. I suspect that, in our enthusiasm, most of us underestimate the significance of this factor; and that, at some time or other, all of us have embarked on intensive therapy more because we wanted to change the client than because he had any incentive or desire for that change. For such client relationship therapy with its more limited goals, and its different techniques, will offer greater opportunities.

Then there is the client's capacity (or lack of it) to verbalize freely his thoughts, and especially his feelings, for the highly intellectualized conversationalist can be as difficult a problem in intensive casework as is his very silent friend. If these deeper feelings can be brought out in action only, our therapeutic techniques must be varied accordingly.

A third criterion is the presence of a serious, and especially an unalterable, reality problem in the client's environment. For, whether we wish it or not, such a reality situation will repeatedly intrude itself into our interviews. How far is it possible—indeed, how far is it ethically justified—to ignore such a situation and need in our concentration on the slow, long-term pattern of our intensive interpretative therapy? And, if we chose to 'deal with' the reality situations, this must surely influence, and modify, our long-term therapeutic goals and intensive techniques.

But perhaps the most important criterion of assessment is the level of emotional and social maturity of the client. Although there are differences, it is legitimate to consider, with the level of maturity, the degree of ego-strength in the client. Let me say at once that my use of the expression 'immaturity' here is as a general clinical guide only; it does not pretend to have the precision of a 'scientific' or accurately measurable term. It is helpful only if we think of immaturity in connection with a particular setting—'immature for which setting'. In the topic now under consideration, it must be the client's level of maturity in terms of capacity for, and experience of, relationships. Even leaving aside those who have been grossly deprived or rejected in childhood, there are many clients whose early experience of relationships was so unsatisfactory that they were never wholly able to work through the initial experience of relationships within the family, the 'give-and-take' of such contacts, the feeling of being approved of, the capacity to internalize controls and standards, and so on. In brief they have failed to mature in this respect. They feel inadequate, and unsure of their contacts; they still see situations narcissistically; they react badly, and often impulsively, to frustration and criticism. Such people will need a parental relationship through which they can experience the relationship patterns they have not had; and thus a parental relationship appropriate to the 'maturity age' which the client has reached. This assessment of maturity level, and of the role needed in the relationship, is often a technically difficult task; and it may require a number of interviews to complete. But it also can be an emotionally very threatening experience for the worker. For the relationship role needed by the client may be greatly at variance with the parental (or perhaps with the 'safer' neutral) role which the worker would like to adopt. Here again is demonstrated the essential need for adequate casework and psychiatric consultation facilities, to say nothing of good basic training, the maturity of the worker herself, and her knowledge of depth psychology.

It would be impossible in the time available to deal in any detail with the techniques of relationship therapy. I intend, therefore, to concentrate on the three major, and closely interconnected, aspects in which our technique differs here from that to which we are accustomed in intensive therapy—the way one uses interpretation; the way one views the transference situation; and the degree to which one can be a 'real person' to the client.

It would be accepted by all of us that we must understand, and become aware of, the unconscious content and motivation of our client's behaviour and reactions; and that one of our important tasks is to give our client insight into these unconscious motivations. It is an interesting comment on a point which I made earlier that some authorities have suggested as alternative titles for intensive therapy such phrases as 'insight-giving therapy' or 'interpretative therapy', as if it were only in this type of therapy that such help is given. I think this confusion arises when we forget that interpretation is a two-stage process; and that considerable latitude of technique, or intensity, is possible in the second stage. The first stage, when we interpret this unconscious material for our own information, and to ourselves as it were, is common to some degree at least to all levels of psychotherapy and casework. But is a detailed verbal interpretation to the client of all this material the only means of providing insight? Do we sometimes interpret in this way for our own intellectual satisfaction rather than because of the client's needs at that moment? Amongst others, Sullivan(2) has had a good deal to say about unnecessary interpretation even in intensive therapy. In appropriate cases can we not provide a worthwhile degree of insight for our client by more indirect means? By our mode of reaction and by what we do? If we accept that our clients in relationship therapy are immature people who will tend to act out rather than verbalize their difficulties, insight may well be better provided by actions rather than by 'intellectualized' verbal explanation; or by simpler verbal methods than we tend to employ in more intensive therapy. Let us take a very simple example from the field of child guidance. A child in the play-room spills sand on to the floor. Our interpretation (to ourselves) is that this is, on this occasion, a trying-out gesture of a child who is unsure of his relationships. In most cases, we do not need to 'explain' this to the child. The way we respond and react will help the client to become aware of the motivation, and to know also that we are aware of (and 'accept') that motivation. With adults the acting out may be more elaborately covered up, but with the type of adult with whom we are dealing here, sensitivity to our response will be as important, and in the long run as productive of insight, as in our example of the child.

I do not intend in any way to minimize the importance of the concept of the transference phenomenon. But have we in recent years come to elaborate its significance too highly and thereby to forget the impact of the reality factors in the situation? Garrett(3) has suggested that before we attribute particular reactions or resistances in a case-work setting to a transference phenomenon, we should first study the reality situation. Has our client been kept waiting, or been given a 'genuinely' inconvenient appointment? Are half her thoughts and attention 'legitimately' at home with her sick child? And so on. Dealing with our present group of clients I would like to go one stage further, and differentiate between capacity for, and experience of, relationships. If our client has had unsatisfactory, or unsatisfying, experience of early parental relationships, clearly this will colour the quality and nature of all his subsequent relationships including that with the therapist. But it will also have made him vulnerable to certain reality situations. He will have been, or felt himself to be, rejected or unwanted or treated 'badly' in all sorts of everyday reality settings. Such reality experiences will be closely linked to transference attitudes, but they will also sensitize him to similar subsequent situations. His reaction to us will often be governed no more by the transference than by the fact he has had 'unfortunate' experiences with a doctor, or a social worker or in another clinic before, and so he visualizes the worker as a threatening reality person and sees himself as if he were in a threatening reality situation. In this type of case we can lose as much by ignoring these reality factors as we should if we ignored the transference phenomenon. I feel that we need to study in much more detail the manipulation (and I use this word in a constructive and ethically proper sense) of the reality setting to the benefit of the client. In brief, we need to appear more as a 'real person' in our interviews with him. This last factor is, I think, the focal point of all our techniques in relationship therapy. Of course, in relationship therapy one does not function as a 'real person', in the way that, say, a close friend or confidant does. Perhaps it would be better to speak of the worker as a 'real professional person'; and, most important of all, we use this 'real-personship' as a deliberate technical skill, through which we help the client.

Even in the most 'passive' setting of the strict psychoanalytical interview, there is a 'feed-back' from therapist to client. Whether we like it or not, one's clients in any interview are assessing one as a person, as well as in the transference setting. As Irvine(4) has suggested, clients with severe disturbances of early relationships may find their phantasy relationships too threatening or frightening to be allowable. For such a client the 'real person' relationship may well be all-important.

When we speak of this type of relationship, we usually think of the worker as functioning in a parental role. Whilst this is a valuable and important concept, it may lead to some confusion unless we are sure of what we mean by a 'parental role'. Surely the important factor will be that the worker functions in that role which (in more fortunate circumstances) the client's parents would have earlier fulfilled, but which these clients have in fact missed. If this is so then the worker will have to function as the 'good parent' does; bearing in mind that the good parent will have to give or withhold, to approve and disapprove, to praise or reprove, according to the real needs of the client, and his capacity to accept such a response at the particular time. (It will not be necessary to stress that it is the client's need, and not the worker's own need, that counts.) It is here that we are using professional skills—and often very expert skills—in our assessment and in our use of the relationship.

Some years ago I was privileged to work with a very experienced psychiatric social worker in one of the earliest experimental community care projects. In our reports on that project,(5) (6) we made special reference to and gave details of this aspect of relationship therapy. Today therefore I propose to mention only those more important points which I feel are worth more skilled consideration and study than we perhaps usually give to them. Yet, if some of us are to work outside the 'safe' atmosphere of the clinic or hospital, and if we are to provide skilled casework consultative or teaching help to workers in allied fields, these are essential technical questions to which we must find the answers.

We say, with much truth, that we can only really help the willing client. Although most of us would be prepared to 'work through' the unconscious resistances of the client, it may be difficult for us to modify our techniques in the face of his conscious, and reality-determined, resistances; or with the client who is compelled to come to us by some legal sanction. In such circumstances, and especially in the crucial first interview, we may sometimes need to be a very 'real person' indeed, a person who can put the reality situation openly to the client. To some of us this may seem the very negation of our accepted technique, yet in some casework settings such as probation or in residental work with adolescents such an initial clarification for ourselves and for our client of our reality authority role may well be an essential preliminary to successful therapy.

For most psychotherapists, and many psychiatric social workers treatment is thought of in terms of regularly spaced interviews over a long period, and held in our own office. But what of the interview on the client's door-step with the door half-closed against us, or on the street corner, or even in the corridor outside our office? In such settings our conventional techniques and roles will need to be varied to make such interviews of value to the client. More study is needed on the value of spacing interviews, on when to work fast and when to leave the problem to 'cook'. Our skills will be taxed to the full in deciding these points, especially in the face of reality crisis situations.

Perhaps the most difficult problems of relationship therapy arise over the provision, or the withholding, of material help. Here the role of the 'good', or 'bad', parent will come into sharp focus; and our insight into our own motivation will come under great strain.

Advice-giving, approval, reproof and reassurance must all be considered in relationship to the client's needs. How best can one show oneself as a real person showing approval of another real person? How else can we build on those (perhaps few) 'positives' that the client shows? How far can we carry this role of the 'real person' without involving ourselves too much in the problem, or with the client?

It will be clear that in relationship therapy, a relatively greater load is carried by the worker, *vis-à-vis* the client's participation, than in interpretative therapy. This may be one reason why some of us are reluctant to enter this field, unless it is because we feel we cannot carry our case-work skills into this type of work.

Let us look at an illustration from an entirely different field. In this lecture I have been using techniques learnt in the practice of psychotherapy. I have used changes of voice tone, of gesture, and of emphasis; and I have varied my phrasing and use of words according to the 'feed-back' from my audience .I have sometimes used questions rather than direct statements. And this because

I have been describing not facts but opinions which for all of us, and even the most insightful of us, have some emotional charging.

I suggest that, in the same vein but in far greater degree, we shall find scope in relationship therapy for those assessment and curative skills that we have learnt in the performance of more interpretative or intensive treatment. I consider that we have a duty to bring these special skills into this field, to refine these for our own use, and to pass them on to those many other workers who in the setting of their work, must deal predominantly with this type of client, who needs such relationship casework or therapy.

References

1. Balint, M. *The Doctor, the Patient and his Illness*, Pitmans Medical Publications, London, 1958.
2. Sullivan, H. S. *Conceptions of Modern Psychiatry*, Tavistock Publications, London, 1955.
3. Garrett, Annette 'The Worker-Client Relationship', *Amer. J. Orthopsychiatry*, Vol. XIX, No. 2, April 1949.
4. Irvine, E. E. 'Transference and Reality in the Casework Relationship', *B.J. Psych. Soc. Work*, Vol. III, No. 4, 1956.
5. Ratcliffe, T. A., and Jones, E. V. *Intensive Casework* in a Community Care Setting, *Case Conference*, Vol. II, No. 10, March, 1956.
6. Ratcliffe, T. A., and Jones, E. V. *Mental Health*, Vol. VIII, Nos 3 and 4, 1949.

Chapter X

The Problem Family
Personality Factors

It is common knowledge amongst workers in the poorer areas of any city that there are very considerable variations in the standards of living, even amongst families which have comparable incomes and comparable housing conditions. This can be seen, on a very superficial and material level, in that some of the houses are better kept and some of the children better dressed, and so on. But the social worker in an area of this type may see the problem at quite a different level. She will know that there are many families where a reasonably stable and secure family life goes on and where the social agencies in the area never come into the picture at all. There are other families which from time to time have need of these social agencies, perhaps because a child has come before the juvenile court, or because of a matrimonial dispute, or for some other problem which requires the help of the agency. But there remain a small number of families in the area which are constantly making demands upon the agencies, which appear to drift from one agency to another seeking help now about this problem, now about that; families which seem to make no progress despite all that the agencies can do for them. It is the members of this group which have come to be known as 'problem families'. (Here it is interesting to note an example of our guilt-driven tendency to run away from something we do not understand by calling it by another name. Into the literature about the problem family is creeping the expression 'under-privileged family'. But let us avoid this side-issue and return to the title of 'the problem family'.)

Obviously, if we are to talk about the 'problem family', we

must have some sort of definition and some terms of reference. I propose to use as a starting-point the definition I have just given, namely that problem families are those which are constantly making demands on the social agencies, which do not seem to make any progress despite the help given to them, and which drift from one agency to another. I am well aware that this definition is by no means a perfect one. For example, it begs one very important question—it raises the issue whether the 'cause' of the problem family may lie in the failure of the social work agencies to provide the right sort of help.

Nevertheless, it is a definition which avoids one pitfall and it has certain advantages for us. It is very easy to argue in a circle about problem families; and I felt that, if I started with a definition which included my own concept of the psychological pattern, there was a danger of doing this very thing so as to 'prove' that that was the right concept after all. Therefore I have deliberately chosen a definition which is purely in terms of the behaviour pattern, the symptom pattern, shown by the problem family. This definition has other advantages; it emphasizes the fact that these problem families have no one symptom. It is not only that different problem families come to the agency with different difficulties; it is that individual problem families come to the various agencies with different problems at different times. They may come first with difficulties of a financial and economic nature; a few months later they may come with a housing difficulty, perhaps because they are unsatisfactory tenants and are threatened with eviction; next, they may contact another agency because one of the children has 'got into trouble', or because the husband has been sent to prison.

I think that this is one of the reasons why so much of the research that has gone into the study of the problem family has been rather unfruitful; for it has tended to think mainly of, and to deal mainly with, the symptoms and the material difficulties of the problem family. What we need to try to do, I suggest, is to find whether there are any underlying psychological factors in the problem family which could bring together these various symptom-reactions into something like a clear-cut, interrelated, understandable pattern. I must emphasize at the outset that all I am trying to do is to suggest certain basic concepts, and to show that these basic concepts have to be considered in relation to the individual nature of the pattern of each individual family. Accepting that these are generalizations, I would suggest for consideration three basic concepts. All three are very closely interrelated, but for clarity I will try to deal with them as separate issues.

First is the concept of immaturity. If we think for a moment of the behaviour of the very young child, the infant, we will realize that he reacts in a certain characteristic way. He very easily becomes angry, tearful or happy, and he swings from one mood to another with great rapidity. He tends to act rather impulsively, and he does not learn from the immediate experiences with which he is faced. We remember that if Johnny, aged three and a half years, wants something, he wants it very badly then and there, and he does not accept frustration very easily.

Now, if we study the behaviour shown by many members of problem families, we see that these people show this same characteristic pattern—the same sort of immature, rather infantile behaviour. They too seem not to learn very much from experience. They change quickly and easily in mood and attitude. They appear to be very susceptible to suggestions and ideas but unable to sustain those ideas for very long; and when they decide that they want a television set, or a washing machine, they tend impulsively to buy it, without giving very much thought to whether they can afford the payments on it or not. In other words it is rather tempting to think, and say, that the behaviour of many of these people is like that of a very young child. One difficulty that arises here, of course, is that these people are *not* three or four years old—they are adult. And therefore, although they are reacting in this very immature way, there is this striking contrast between their actual age and their behaviour. Herein I suggest lies one of the central difficulties we have to face, and with which we have to cope, in dealing with the problem family. I do not recall that anyone has done a large-scale research into the intellectual level of members of problem families; but I suspect that very often what workers have regarded as intellectual backwardness is really this pattern of immature behaviour appearing so much out of keeping with 'what one would expect from people of that age'.

Let us, then, consider in rather more detail this concept of immaturity. We can accept that everyone, in the course of his or her development, goes through certain quite well-recognized stages of development. Many of these stages we can observe in infants and children: the way in which the child gradually comes to accept frustration, begins to be able to share things and gradually becomes more of a 'socialized' person. We see him giving way less and less to his basic instinctual desires; we see the way in which he gradually begins to conform to the requirements of society, in that there are certain things which he can do and certain things which he cannot do.

It seems that the members of these problem families have not progressed very far along this line of developing maturity. It is as though they have never reached an 'adult' level of psychological, emotional and social development. But the block has not always been at exactly the same point, for I am not suggesting that all members of all problem families are at the same level of immaturity. Not only are some more generally immature than others, but I believe that individual members vary in maturity and in their capacity for mature decisions and mature reactions, in different spheres and roles. Similarly, the various members of a problem family are not all equally immature. My own clinical impression (and I do not know how far this is confirmed by others) is that there is often a very considerable disparity in the level of immaturity between, for example, husband and wife in the problem family. I have the impression that the wife, though still immature, is often a little more mature than her husband; and that, in this sort of situation, the husband takes on much more the role of one of the children than the role of husband and breadwinner. What is even more important is that capacity to perform any role as a member of the family will vary according to the individual's maturity. For example, one of the characteristics of the very immature person is his difficulty in visualizing his own 'separateness'; in seeing other people as individuals in their own right. He thinks of others much more as a part, an 'extension', of himself; and of his relationships with others in the same 'possessive' sense. Now the newly-born infant has this same need to 'belong'; this same need to feel his mother as a part of himself. So in her role as the mother of a small infant the mother in the problem family may be functioning at a satisfactory level. Her very immaturity may enable her to provide for much of the infant's emotional needs. In that sector of her motherhood role, she may be 'successful'; but it will be a very different matter when we come to consider her capacity in other spheres of motherhood. She may well prove quite ineffectual in her methods of feeding or clothing the baby; she may not even organize her budget efficiently enough to buy suitable, or sufficient, food or clothing for the infant. And she will certainly find it much more difficult to handle, and be much more unable to tolerate, the stage of growing independence in the child—or for that matter the independence of her husband. It is this type of disparity which can be so puzzling to the worker with the problem family, unless she sees it in terms of varying roles, and varying levels of maturity in coping with these roles.

If we study the history of these members of the problem family, the pattern of their own childhood and the experiences which they have had in life, we can, I think, understand more clearly the reasons for their immaturity. In my experience, very few of these people have been completely deprived emotionally, in the sense of never having any mother-relationship at all; but many of them have a childhood background of much insecurity. They have received some mothering and mother-love; but they have experienced an unstable pattern of handling and attitudes with no very clear-cut relationship within which the child could identify and mould himself. They have known no really emotionally secure setting in which they could develop beyond a certain stage of maturity. In other words, their background and developmental history were such as could be expected to result in this degree of social and emotional immaturity.

The second concept (which is closely linked with the first) concerns the type of relationship pattern which occurs in the problem family. Characteristically, these people find it difficult to accept that, in their relationship with others, there must be an element of giving and taking. They tend to view relationships solely in the sense of what they themselves receive. Their relationship pattern is essentially self-centred. Again it reminds us of the sort of relationships which we see in very young children; they are wholly possessive, because the child has not yet reached the stage where he realizes that he must both give and take, and share his relationships within the group. So here too in their pattern of relationships we find further evidence of the immaturity of these individuals. If we consider this aspect in more detail much of importance emerges.

Now it is an obvious, but none the less significant fact that the problem family, or indeed any other family unit, does not consist of isolated people living in a sort of vacuum. These individual people are living together as a unit, and have therefore relationship-patterns with each other. Thus in the problem family we have a situation in which each member is unable to form a mature giving and taking relationship with the other family members. Inevitably, such meagre relationships as do exist come under new and further stress and strain from this source, and are increasingly likely to break down.

I remember how one of the very first patients whom I treated at great length, quite a few years ago, responded to treatment in a way which was (I felt in those days) a personal triumph. She was an anxious, worried woman, who was afraid of making social contacts. We reached the stage where she had become much more confident, much more mature and capable of making social contacts. I was feeling extremely pleased with myself. One evening, towards the end of this long period of treatment her husband came to collect her after our interview. He spoke to me for a few minutes and said: 'Well, I must admit you seem to have cured my wife, but you have given me a hell of a life in return, because now she wants to go out to some social function every evening!' The moral of this story is something we are very apt to forget when thinking of problem families: that is, the interaction of the members of the family towards each other. Anything which changes the pattern of one member not only affects that particular member of the family but will affect the other people in the family also. To give another example, the mother in a problem family, as I have already said, often copes surprisingly well with her children whilst they are very young, partly because the children are dependent on her and thus she can fulfil this rather primitive motherhood role of being protector to her children. But as the children grow older the immature mother finds it much more difficult to tolerate the situation. She begins to feel insecure. She becomes subject to new stresses and this in turn makes its impact upon the husband, and so on. Thus, an interacting pattern of relationships and behaviour is something of tremendous influence and significance to the whole family.

Again, if the husband is functioning more in the role of one of the children, dependent on the slightly more mature wife, she in turn will obtain a certain amount of satisfaction by being protective. But she may find it much harder to see, or accept, her husband in his role as a breadwinner. She may find it very difficult to tolerate him earning or working. As a result he may be unable to cope with difficulties in that setting. He may lose his job, or have a poor work record, and that in turn will reflect back again upon the family. These difficulties have to be sorted out. We must consider not just the personality pattern of each member of the family, but the way in which these personalities interact on one another.

Let us now consider the third concept. If you were an immature person who had had no stable background; if in your own childhood the very first set of relationships which you had experienced, namely with mother and father, had not worked out satisfactorily; and if, for one reason or another, you had not been able to build on that foundation a secure pattern of human relationships, you would go through life still unsure of those relationships. You would still seek relationships into which you would 'fit'; or would view new relationships rather suspiciously. Moreover this difficulty can be perpetuated, and accentuated, by the attitude of the community. For there are many times when such people are faced with situations in which they are made to feel inferior; in which they feel criticized; in which they are outcasts and unwanted.

Some years ago I took part in a research project studying the problem of men who had very bad employment records, to discover what help was possible for them. One striking thing about the clients who came to us was that almost all of them were described by the referring social work agencies as being people who were 'not worth while'. There were reports like 'This man is quite a useless person'; 'I have rarely seen a man less prepared to help himself'. Throughout many of these referral reports was this intense criticism. It is not therefore surprising that these people, who are already unsure of their relationships and unable to make satisfactory mature contacts, feel that such experiences have intensified over and over again their basic insecurity. Inevitably they become more and more vulnerable.

If for example the mother from a problem family has to go into hospital and something accidentally goes wrong with the admission arrangements (as can occur even in the best hospitals) that mother may well feel that she is being 'hit at' personally because the authorities have a down on her. Yet this vulnerability goes back really to the experiences of her childhood and the previous repetition of similar experiences. The incident in hospital is only one link in the whole chain of incidents and attitudes. Here is an important lesson for all who come into contact with these individuals.

Yet so often the problem family is seen only as a unit which demands and takes, a unit which takes help from a social agency and then disappears, only to re-appear soon with fresh demands. In these circumstances it is so dangerously easy for the worker to feel hurt; to feel that there is no 'gratitude'; to view the family as 'not worth while'; to miss seeing this as a failure in the pattern of primary human relationships.

This same difficulty extends into other fields. For example, the husband who comes into contact with his workmates and with the foreman in charge of his group; but, just as he is unable to form satisfactory human relationships within his own family group, equally he cannot make mature or stable contacts within his work group. Perhaps he finds great difficulty in accepting authority, or he is suspicious of help, or he is so immature that he cannot make a satisfactory contact unless things go all his own way. The result of these circumstances is that the husband begins to have a poor employment record; he loses job after job. As a consequence the family get into economic and financial difficulties and that again reflects back on the structure of the family. They go to the Welfare Services or to a social agency and are told: 'We gave you all that assistance last week. Where has it all gone?' So again the whole cycle is intensified.

It would be interesting to speculate, at this point, how far this expression—'the problem family'—has come to be regarded as meaning that such families are a problem to the social work agency, almost a nuisance to the agency, rather than a problem to and within themselves; and how far this attitude has tended to intensify these very difficulties which I have just described.

It seems to me therefore that if we are adequately to study the psychological pattern of the problem family, we must think of this pattern in various 'layers'. Our first 'layer' would be represented by the individual members of the problem family; by the level of psychological, emotional and social development which they have reached. Then secondly we must think of the impact which each particular person has on the other members of the family, and they on him. The final 'layer' is the contact of that family with other people in the community and, quite as important, the impact of the community's attitude on the family.

Now, because of this pattern of immaturity which, I suggest, is the fundamental concept, it is relatively uncommon in my experience for members of a problem family to show actual neurotic symptoms. Whilst we should, perhaps, be very careful to define exactly what we mean by these terms, I can only describe this aspect briefly and in somewhat simplified form. It is, I think, that these people have not developed to such a stage of emotional and social growth that there is any great conflict between their instinctive, primitive wishes, desires and urges and any sort of inner, personal control. They are not subject to the same type of deeper conflict as is the more mature person; and therefore (again oversimplifying very much) there is not the same need for them to develop neurotic defences. I suggest that this is important, for it affects the whole question of treatment and help for these families.

The more experience I have had over quite a number of years with problem families the more I have been struck by one feature, which may come as a surprise to many, as it did to me initially. The more one studies the problem family in the light of the aetiological and psychodynamic patterns the more one is impressed by the potential strengths of these family units, and of their individual members. The strengths may be (and indeed almost always are) very limited, but some potential is there. These people are grossly immature; but they have made some progress up the ladder of emotional and social growth. In my experience, one rarely sees the true psychopathic personality in the problem family. Few problem family members are so completely and fully deprived, so much withdrawn into their 'shell', that they are unable to form any relationships at all. There remains some capacity for relationships, given the right therapeutic setting;

there is some potential strength. And these are the only useful foundations on which we can hope to build.

What does all this mean and imply for us, either in our capacity as citizens or in whatever role we occupy in the fields of social work or psychiatry? First and most important is something very obvious though it still requires emphasis. It is that problem families do consist of individual people who have their own pattern of interacting with each other. This is a very obvious statement, yet so often, I think, legislation and the community adopt an attitude to the problem family which seems to deny this concept. So often the problem is thought of far more in terms of material benefits, help and welfare. I am not belittling in any way the importance of material help, which is often essential. But what I would stress is that their handicaps are not just material; it is not just material help that matters. In other words, if we are to 'cure' the problem family, we shall not succeed in doing so by any form of material or financial help alone. These things may be valuable and necessary, but they will deal merely with the symptoms. I suggest that we must do some re-thinking in terms of the legislative attitudes towards the problem family. For in the long run these attitudes mean yours and mine as citizens. For example a great deal of time, energy, earnest endeavour and money is poured out in removing children from 'problem family' homes, on the grounds that the parents are unable to look after them and therefore these children would be better brought up under a pattern which is materially better, where they could be better fed, clothed and housed. But we have to ask ourselves seriously: is this a policy which aims at curing the symptoms, or at really helping the problem family? Some workers believe that, since problem families have too many children anyway, the obvious thing is to get the mother to a birth-control clinic at the earliest possible opportunity and so reduce the risk of further increase. There is no doubt that if there are, say, five children under seven years of age in a household, there will be many more reality problems; and this means that the immature mother will not be able to look after them so well. But, can we deal with such a problem symptomatically? If by persuading the mother to go to the birth-control clinic she is prevented from using her whole central function, namely that of being a mother, what will be the impact of this on her? What will be the impact of that mother's reaction on the father? When we come to think of rehousing these families, or giving them greater financial assistance, we must again consider the emotional impact of such help. All these aids may be necessary in certain circumstances but they are only treating the symptom. What I am suggesting is that we must consider and work out these underlying factors in the problem family, so that we can adequately deal not only with the symptoms, but with these underlying factors, with the actual people themselves.

There is another aspect which we must also consider, though perhaps it is a rather unpopular one for some of us. A great deal of research has been carried out, but most of it has been from the medico-social rather than from the psychological angle. Yet there is scope here for a great deal of extremely important research in the complete study of the problem family; of its inter-relationship patterns, its levels of maturity; of the concepts I have described. For these concepts are based on clinical observations only. I happen to think these views are sound and true, but there is not at the moment adequate research to 'prove' their truth. And since I am suggesting that we should think in terms which imply modifying social and community attitudes and possibly influencing legislation, we must first validate these observations by research. It will be an extremely difficult research project, if it is adequately to cover the complex interplay of psychological, social and economic factors involved. It is research that will involve the sociologist, the caseworker, the cultural anthropologist, the psychiatrist, and others too. And it is not irrelevant to comment here that, unless these various specialists can first learn to work together as a team, they will not present a very satisfactory model of relationships for the problem family itself.

These concepts have another implication for us: there is the question of treatment for these families. It seems to me that if we accept the view that the problem family's real difficulty is a primary failure of human relationships, then the only way in which we can hope to modify the situation is by providing these people with some form of satisfactory relationship therapy. In other words we must provide for them, in a therapeutic setting, the experience of a relationship which they can come to rely upon, to trust and to use as the foundation for their future relationships with other people. This means that the therapeutic relationship must be handled at a very high level of skill and understanding and with full insight into the underlying problem. If, then, these concepts and ideas are true, the main task of therapy lies with the caseworker. Casework must always be a skilled professional task, based on high standards of training and understanding. But it is perhaps in work with problem families, more than in any other field, that the caseworker will have to use special skills in an especially difficult setting. Her aim will be to provide that type of therapeutic relationship within which the individual member of the problem family can mature and discover that possibilities of more satisfactory human relationships can exist for him. This will be a slow and laborious process, expensive in manpower and money. There will be no spectacular results, and the present generation of problem families may make only a short step forward. But even such a step will have its influence on the next generation. It must be a long-term project.

I suggest then that material help—housing, financial help, birth control clinics, and other similar things—must be geared into this therapeutic casework approach. They have all to be part and parcel of that approach, if we are to get anywhere at all. Let us try to see problem families not just as a problem to ourselves as social workers, psychiatrists, magistrates and citizens—but let us try to see the underlying problems of the families themselves, to appreciate that the problem family consists of individual people and individual personalities, interacting with each other and with the community as a whole. Only when we begin to explore that concept—and there is so much still to explore—can we really hope to get down to the basic problem of building up these families and achieving, not in our generation perhaps but eventually, the eradication of these difficulties from the community.

Chapter XI

Specific Aspects of Health Education Preventive Mental Health for the Teacher and Doctor

Some initial explanation is necessary since I do not propose to deal with mental health in its narrow sense. I know of no convincing evidence to show that any preventive measures can significantly reduce the incidence of serious mental illness. But there is considerable evidence to show that satisfactory child-rearing methods can do much to aid good maturation and the growth towards good citizenship. These are the aspects which I would like to discuss today.

But of course this is a vast subject which would justify a whole conference in its own right; indeed, like some of my colleagues, I have taken part in many such conferences on this topic during the past years and in various areas of the country, as part of the in-service training of teachers, doctors, health visitors and the like. Today I have only half an hour: consequently, if you say afterwards that I have missed out a great deal, generalized on many topics and sometimes been provocative, you will be quite right. My aim has not been to attempt to cover the whole subject, but rather to help your thinking and discussion on these problems. Which, incidentally, we could take as quite a good slogan for health education in general, and mental health education in particular.

There are three separate but interrelated areas in which the two professions mainly represented here today impinge upon this problem—in our contact with parents individually, in group situations or as members of the community; in our contact with children; and in our task of training student members of our two professions. This conference is concerned mainly with the third of these, but we can only fully understand that aspect by considering first the other two areas of contact.

Our two professions are very fond of 'giving advice', and it is always described as 'good advice'—unless of course someone else gives it! Now there is nothing wrong with advice as such, and it is reasonable to suppose that the professionally trained individual may well have more expert knowledge in his field than has the lay person whom he comes to help. But is our advice *always* good, realistic and really meant to help the client? How often do we give advice *only* because the client really needs our advice at that time?

To consider our first point: is our advice always realistic and practicable for the client? Or, to put it another way, do we listen to the problem and to the client adequately before we give our advice? Nowadays, we may no longer make such blatant mistakes as the eminent physician who, in the 1930 depression era, used to advise his bronchitic (and often unemployed) out-patients with great earnestness that they should winter in Egypt or the South of France. But in less obvious ways we can be (and often are) equally unrealistic. How often are parents advised never to quarrel in front of their children, never to be cross and so on? And since such advice is impracticable of achievement in real life, how guilty, unsure and anxious will the 'good' parent become through his, or her, 'failure' to achieve these impossible standards. My own professional experience shows that this parental unsureness and sense of failure will be much more damaging to the child than ever would be the occasional quarrels or necessary firm reprimand. We could all give many other similar examples.

When parents bring a problem to us do we listen adequately first, or do we jump in at once with our 'ready-made' (as opposed to 'made-to-measure', if we may continue the analogy) solution? Quite apart from the great therapeutic value to the parents themselves of being listened to understandingly, unless we listen adequately how can we hope to know what the problem really is; and even more importantly how can we hope to discover what the sufferer thinks or feels about the problem, or what it means to him?

Then again, our professional advice so often tends to be dogmatic, and to be given on a take-or-leave it, the-expert-has-spoken basis. One is remainded of the constant cry of the accuser in medieval heresy trials: 'I am not concerned with what you think about these matters. I am concerned only with what I tell you—you must believe.' It is small wonder that such advice, so given, can produce an intense sense of failure and inadequacy in the recipient, rather than provide relief.

Moreover, are our expert views always so right and infallible? When I was first training as a paediatrician, one of my chiefs was an ardent supporter of the rigidly scheduled and carefully timed feeding of infants; the other was one of the earliest exponents of 'on-demand' feeding. Each preached his own view with a degree of conviction which must have made any mother who acted against his advice feel that she was taking very grave risks about her baby's health. Which of the two was giving the 'correct advice'? What confusion and uncertainty must such divergent, but dogmatic, opinions have produced for these mothers—to say nothing of the poor house physician who had always to be alert to worship the right gods at the right time!

Then again we tend often to 'over-sell' opinions and advice. For example, one of the major advances in preventive mental health has been the work of Bowlby and his associates on the importance of the mother-infant relationship. Yet this too can be (and nowadays often is) stressed to such a degree that many good mothers anxiously and guiltily anticipate grave damage to their child through those brief, but inevitable, separations which must occur in every child's life. It has been oversold also to the point of diminishing the equally valuable and essential role of the father *vis-à-vis* the child.

I am not suggesting that many of these views are not soundly based; or that advice should never be given. But surely if it is to be of real value advice must be tailored to the parents' needs; and to their potential and their limitations. Mental health is about real people; and maturity and good citizenship do not consist in reaching some theoretical level of perfection. The aim must be to help each individual to make as good an adjustment as his potential and circumstances will allow; and to take it confidently, and in the way most suitable for him.

If our tendency is to be too authoritarian in our professional contact with parents, the reverse is often true when we are faced with the child as an individual or in a group. Why are we so often reluctant to be that confident, definite and reliable adult figure which the child (and the adolescent too for that matter) so urgently needs, and so often seeks, if in indirect ways? In this day and age we can become so obsessed with 'theory' that we fail to recognize the reality and everyday factors. If a child is being difficult in class, it is a dangerously easy evasion of one's adult responsibility to assume at once that there is some deep psychological cause—and to forget that it might be due to our own failure to control (or interest) the class; or because Johnnie was being deliberately provocative just for the fun of it!

I have left myself only a short time to deal with the third theme —what are we to teach our students in this field? Fortunately, all that I have already said is relevant to this final theme. All I need provide, therefore, would be some suggestions for the essential content of such training.

Although a knowledge of the mechanisms which lie behind, and beneath, human behaviour is of immense value to any student whose work lies with people, a too rigid love of theory unrelated to its practical application has often bedevilled the task of giving help to those in need. It may be valuable (or, for the specialist, essential) to know that a child has (say) an 'oedipal conflict', and to be aware of the complex motivation behind this. But the possession of this theoretical knowledge alone will not get us far towards helping the child; or relieving his distress. It may be useful to know the theoretical motivation for one's child's temper-tantrum—but the actual tantrum, and the child, still have to be handled. And you cannot do that at a 'theoretical' level!

An equally important balance to achieve lies between the study of 'normal' and 'abnormal' behaviour. Obviously we cannot, and should not, ignore the existence of serious emotional disturbance; but the majority by far of those children with whom your students will come in contact will be essentially normal. I was recently told by a lecturer in education at a college of education, with great sincerity, that he had always emphasized to his students that there 'were no naughty children, only emotionally sick children'. Hearing this, I wondered how his students would feel, and cope, when they were faced with their first class of normally provocative children who were determinedly 'trying out' their new teacher to see how far they could go?

To achieve these two essential, and other similar, balances seems to me to require as much the right choice of lecturers on these topics as the choice of suitable content in the course itself. In brief, let the subject of human growth and development be described in terms of real children in real situations, and given therefore by someone with experience in working with such real children.

Above all let us remember that only the really mature professional worker (whether student or lecturer) who has come realistically to terms with his own feelings and prejudices, can help with the problems of others. How far does our training policy and practice help, or delay, this maturation in our students?

This is perhaps, the most important point that I can leave with you.

Chapter XII

Community Mental Health in Practice[1]

It must always be a valued privilege to speak to a National Association for Mental Health Conference; but I am especially grateful for this privilege on the present occasion, when this year so much emphasis is being laid on the practical aspects of our mental health task. And, as a token of that emphasis there is the attempt to increase the feeling of participation in the conference by all of us, in the discussion groups which are to follow. But I am very aware also of the responsibilities of my position. Not only have I to try to follow two very distinguished people, but I have also to prepare the way for the four experts who are to speak next. They will be giving you the practical aspects of their particular sections of the mental health field, from the wealth of their experience and skill.

It is for me, then, to paint in the general background, leaving the detail brushwork to those who follow and the final criticism and appraisal of the picture to your discussion groups.

The concept of mental health in a community would seem to demand two things—that individual members of that community should be themselves stable, secure and settled; and that the community pattern itself should be a mentally healthy one. Thus the presence of the socially maladjusted, the social misfit, looms large in the problem of community mental health. The delinquent, the chronic absentee from industry, the problem family, the solitary and inadequate personality type and the many other members of this group are not only a constant challenge to our

[1] Note: This lecture was originally delivered at an NAMH Conference in 1949. For reasons given in the Author's Introductory Note, it is printed here in its original form and without any alterations.

preventive and curative skills but the barometer of our social climate and an indication of the community's health or ill-health. It is for this reason that I want to use the practical study of this group as a foundation for my survey of community mental health.

There was a once commonly used phrase: 'the poor and needy'. Often one heard it used in a derogatory or jocular way, but today I am going to use it quite seriously and carefully. For it does emphasize what is a most important point: the poor and the needy are not essentially the same people. The poor are by no means always the unstable; and one who is in great need of help of social adjustment may be well provided for in the material sense. In other words the provision of material rewards and security is of itself *alone* not sufficient to ensure social and emotional security. I do not deny in any way the importance of economic security and freedom from want—their essential value to a community's well-being goes without saying—but it seems that we are in danger of regarding material security as the only factor in community care needed to produce a socially healthy nation.

If we examine English social history and legislation during the past 100 years, we will see how much emphasis was first laid on the improvement of material factors—using the word material here in its widest sense. That this was so was inevitable and necessary for no other social approach could have helped until the gross evils of acute widespread poverty and want, the factory and working conditions of the Industrial Revolution and the entire lack of public health measures (to name only the major and early evils) had been eliminated. Gradually legislation has come to consider other aspects than the purely material, but even the most recent of social legislation is heavily weighted in its interpretation towards the material side. Our attitude towards a National Health Service, for example, has concentrated so much on the provision of material and physical requirements that we have largely forgotten the importance of the patient-doctor relationship—or for that matter the importance of good professional-administrative relationships. The Curtiss Committee, I feel sure, were only too well aware of the emotional problems of the deprived child, but to some local authorities the interpretation of the Children's Act has been limited to the better provision of good physical care of the deprived child. In so many discussions of the problem of juvenile delinquency we will hear so much stress laid on material factors—poverty, the provision of youth clubs and so on—how widely is the emotional pattern of the delinquent child understood and considered?

In our consideration of the problems of productivity and industrial absenteeism we talk a great deal of economic incentives. How much importance do we allot to the more imponderable factors of industrial morale or the dynamics of human relationships?

If absenteeism, delinquency, low industrial morale, chronic minor ill-health, divorce, child neglect and other similar problems are to be regarded as symptoms of social ill-health, how important is it for us to clarify our ideas on the positive social health factors which will prevent these symptoms? How far are we, as workers in the field of mental health, dealing with these symptoms at an administrative or a professional level?

Because this is essentially a joint conference of both administrators and workers in the clinical field, I do not want to deal today with the purely psychiatric aspects of the problem. There are still, of course, many shortcomings in our hospital psychiatric services; sometimes these shortcomings are appreciated and valiant efforts are made to overcome them in the face of many inevitable post-war shortages. But sometimes, unfortunately, even the existence of these shortcomings is not accepted or understood. And there remain many sufferers from mental ill-health—in the widest sense of the word—who do not fall within the province of the orthodox psychiatric clinic—the socially maladjusted to whom I have just referred. How much can, or should, this group become the province of the expert in mental health?

Perhaps the largest single experiment in this field has been the work of the National Association for Mental Health Community

Care Service; and I think we can learn something from its experience. Started as a regional after-care scheme for men invalided from the Forces with psychiatric disability, it slowly developed into a comprehensive community care service dealing essentially with the social misfit and the socially maladjusted. There is no time today to describe its work in detail, but let us consider briefly these major aspects of its work—its methods, its results and its justification as an independent treatment service in its own right.

Those of us especially who have experience of child guidance work know of the value of psychiatric team work with its carefully integrated treatment approach to all the tangled aspects of the problem, each worker's approach offering its own special skills and methods, but complementing each other to produce a total benefit to the patient that no one of the team could give singly. This team principle—in this case by psychiatrist, psychiatric social worker and social worker—is used in the National Association for Mental Health community care work also, but with this important difference; the psychiatric social worker and social worker assume the major therapeutic role. It is her interviews with the client which are the essential part of the treatment process, the psychiatrist leaving his more orthodox role to become a technical advisor and co-ordinator in the background. His presence, support and skill are essential to the team but whilst he may have occasional interviews with the client, it is the psychiatric social worker who works through the client's tensions and difficulties in her therapeutically planned series of interviews. What is the process at work in these interviews?

One can—and indeed one does—explain it in terms of depth psychology, but for our present purpose let us consider it more simply as 'relationship therapy'—the impact of one human being on another handled with the special skills and experience with which the psychiatric social worker is trained. Whatever its cause, whatever its complex intertwined symptoms, the one common factor of all socially maladjusted people is their inability, to a greater or a lesser degree, to form adequate stable or satisfactory human relationships with others in their environment. And in the community care technique the socially maladjusted is faced for the first time with the possibility of a stable, secure understanding, warm, and yet at the same time, passive, human relationship with the psychiatric social worker. Very, very slowly will this relationship build up; the psychiatric social worker will have to face many interviews, resentment and often open hostility, over-dependence and over-demanding attitudes and the inevitable ups and downs of such a budding relationship. But more importantly she will have to deal skilfully with each phase as it arises, just as the wise mother will deal with each similar phase in her gradually developing relationship with her child. And just as the parent-child relationship should be the epitome of future relationships for the child and the path which leads him on to adult maturity and independence of personality, so the client-psychiatric social worker relationship should be an experience which leads the client on until he can form his own mature adult relationships in his environment. It is not a relationship in which the aim is a dependency of the client on the psychiatric social worker in either the material or the emotional sense. It is rather an educative process towards mature independence. The whole time she is building up her relationship the psychiatric social worker is working also to make the client ultimately no longer need her support. And therein this special technique of relationship therapy differs from the technique of more orthodox social work. It is a deep human relationship and not one in any sense dependent on material support or provision. It differs too from the narrow and more conventional psychotherapies in that it is dealing with the individual in the actual milieu of his environment rather than in the artificial isolation of the clinic or consulting room.

It is a technique, then, which is intended more for the individual who reacts to his own inner difficulties by anti-social patterns than for one whose symptomatic reactions are contained within himself; more, in short, for the personality disturbance than for the frankly neurotic. That these two groups overlap and intertwine is indisputable, but if we are frank enough to face up to the realities of situation we will admit that even the best staffed psychiatric clinics can at present handle only the most hopeful fringe of the neurotic group. For the rest many hours of manpower and vast sums of money are spent by industry and by the state coping in a symptomatic stop-gap way with the results of social maladaptation, but doing little to get to the root causes of the problem. It is, in the light of this failure of stop-gap methods, that we must assess the value of community care techniques, as a separate entity from the more orthodox psychiatric services.

Recently there was carried out under the auspices of the National Association for Mental Health, a careful detailed survey in depth of a group of individuals under community care. The numbers were of necessity small and I do not quote them as statistics; but of this group of thirty men and women, all with grossly unstable work records, twenty-four were helped to a worthwhile degree and four others to a lesser degree. And this, remember, is in a group who were deliberately chosen as the 'hopeless failures' of more orthodox and established methods, and in an area, too, where in general the existing psychiatric and social services were of above average ability compared to the country as a whole.

Community care of this type remains within the province of the local health authority. Shorn—and I think unfortunately shorn—of so much of its responsibility for health services by the Act, here surely remains an opportunity to work up a worthwhile health service and a challenge to each local health authority to do a better job than their neighbours. Some local authorities have accepted that challenge and begun the slow but steady building up of a real community care service. But to many others the opportunities of the Act have meant merely an extension—and not always an improvement—of their existing duly authorized officer activities.

Of course, the community care technique has its difficulties—

and great difficulties they are too. It is, for one thing, an immensely time-consuming technique; each client will require many hours of skilled social worker time and the development of an adequate relationship is something which cannot and must not be hurried. But is it so very time-consuming when we compare it to the existing wastage of man-hours from absenteeism in industry, to the repeated and often fruitless efforts of various social agencies with the problem family, to the overcrowded doctor's surgery and the cost of medicines for so much minor ill-health or, for that matter, to the human misery, unhappiness or want which is so often the portion of the maladjusted and his family? And if these maladjustments are symptoms of faulty human relationships, how else can we hope to deal with them except through the medium of the dynamic psychology of such relationships?

Let us consider some examples at quite a simple and superficial level of the importance of human beings in terms of individual relationship problems rather than as mere ciphers in the mass of the community.

Some years ago a cosmetic firm decided to give to each member of its staff a box of cosmetics as a present to celebrate the firm's anniversary year. Each of its staff was asked to say which particular shade of cosmetics she used. But when the time came there was no such individual distribution: in one department all the boxes were of one cosmetic shade; in another department another bulk distribution of boxes all of another shade. Thus, except to the few, the gift was useless—and even the few were only satisfied by accident as it were. The material gift was there all right; so was the idea behind the gift. But a total failure to treat the employees as individuals meant that the gift, far from improving factory morale, greatly worsened it.

In a recent discussion with a group of works foremen, the question was raised as to how often absenteeism was due to individual social problems. The general reply was surprising—that very few of those foremen had ever thought of assessing or investigating that side of the problem. We talk, perhaps rather glibly, of major material factors in absenteeism which affect whole masses of people, but shall we ever really assess the problem or cure it until we get down to the dynamics of the individual in his relationship to his total environment, until we get down to the real emotional factors which are keeping that particular individual a chronic absentee. And we must remember that these basic factors are often in fields of his social environment quite remote from work. To give but one example the psychological conflicts of a deep-seated marital incompatability may be as potent a factor in altering a man's attitude to work as may bad factory conditions. And no amount of material help alone will affect this problem. Only a skilled, careful study of the individual's relationship with his total social environment and an equally careful and skilled handling of the results can deal adequately with the social ill-health of absenteeism, chronic minor ill-health, juvenile delinquency and the rest.

I have emphasized the word 'skilled', for here lies our second great difficulty. I do not need to tell you of the shortage of skilled workers in the mental health field, and especially of psychiatric social workers. But are we all doing all we can to remedy this shortage? Have we all accorded the psychiatric social worker the professional status she deserves as one of the key-workers in the mental health programme—or pressed for her to be paid a salary comparable with that status? A recent correspondence in the papers has rather highlighted the occasions when the unskilled worker may be paid more than the skilled. And for that matter has anyone yet agreed what the exact function and training of the psychiatric social worker can or should be?

Community care methods call for special skills and training which are at present almost the prerogative of the psychiatric social worker. But in any long term view, it is clear that these vast problems of community ill-health must be the province of the social workers already in the field, the family case worker, the probation officer, the industrial welfare worker and so on. How far are these two prospects compatible?

If you are going to produce any article in quantity—whether it is a motor car or a drawing pin—you must first have your skilled designers, you jigs and your machine tools. And even when your production machinery is in full swing you must still have your technician and skilled overseer to eradicate production errors, to improve output results and to promote smooth running. The man operating the lathe need not be a master-craftsman with a detailed skill in the design and building of lathes, but he must be knowledgeable in how and why the lathe works, capable and efficient in working it and able and ready to call in the expert technician's help when necessary. Both technician and operative have an essential place in the team, through which the basic skills and training of the technician are blended with the special knowledge and experience of the individual worker in his individual task, to produce the finished product. Let us translate this analogy into our own sphere of social work.

It seems to me unnecessary—and it is certainly impracticable—to suggest that all social workers in all fields should be trained as skilled therapists or with the full and special techniques of the psychiatric social worker. Detailed diagnosis and treatment of the gravely disturbed individual must always remain the province of the specialist technician in that field. But the general social worker is the operative of the social health machine and she must be equipped and trained to that level. She must know broadly how and why that machine works, why it goes wrong and how to deal with or prevent its simpler failures and how the task of her individual part of the machine fits into the total pattern of social health.

In this country the training of the qualified social worker in her own particular type of work is usually good, but it is time we recognized that for all forms of social work adequate training is necessary. We still see too often the advertisement which ends—'training or experience in social work will be an advantage but is not essential'. Yet how far is even the qualified social worker trained in what should be the essential foundations of her skill, a knowledge of the dynamics of human relationships and the importance of the individual emotional factor in social maladjustments? Without that knowledge how can she know why the machinery of her clinical case work is running—or why it has broken down, skilled though she is in the technicalities of her own particular field of social work?

The task of the expert in mental health is thus surely like that of the factory technician and a threefold one. He must work out in his own clinical and social experience the designs and dynamics of the problem of human relationships; he must be prepared to step in with diagnosis and skilled help if a machine breaks down so severely that the social worker-operative cannot deal with it. And, perhaps most important of all, he must have a big part in training the social worker-operative of each machine in the simpler dynamics and care of her machine.

Two universities to my knowledge—and no doubt others also—have shown the possibilities and value of teaching to all their social science students the significance of this psychiatric approach. Much remains to be done in the proper selection and education of all social workers, but this must be a province where the mental health expert has his say. Just as full production of any material article is impossible without the combination of machine-tool and machine that uses it, of specialist technician and skilled operative, so does the mass attack necessary to tackle the massive problem of social ill-health need the combination of mental health expert and clinical case-worker.

What then can the local authority do to build up a real mental health community service? Much of the detail of both the possibilities and the limitations of such a programme will best be dealt with in your discussion groups today and tomorrow, but there are points I would like to put to you now for your consideration. Ideally your team must consist of psychiatrist and psychiatric social workers functioning in close collaboration with all the available social services, voluntary and statutory, in your area, with close and personal links with the psychiatric clinics, probation, family welfare organizations, Ministry of Labour, the local health services and many others. I would warmly commend to your study the 1949 Report of the Leeds Mental Health Service, as a description of what possibilities there are for such active work under Section 28 of the Act.

But even where a complete team approach is not possible, there still remains much that can be done, whilst aiming always at the ultimate goal of the full psychiatric team. With the help of even only one skilled mental health technician, psychiatrist or psychiatric social worker, every local authority could utilize for this purpose its wealth of good general case workers. Your health visitor, your children's department, your probation officers, your workers in the maternity and child welfare clinics have all access to, and must be given an interest in, the field of preventive mental health. They are the workers who meet the problem in the community; they must be the real operatives of the mental health machine. They must be linked with your existing facilities, your child guidance and psychiatric clinics, your duly authorized officer service, your embryo community care organization so that each can come to understand and value the work of the others. So that there is slowly built up throughout your whole welfare services, an understanding of what I have called 'the psychiatric approach' to social case work and social problems. So that your mental health department becomes a closely integrated part of a real total community service.

Let us therefore consider briefly what we mean by 'the psychiatric approach'.

First, it is based on knowledge of the mechanisms of human behaviour and the importance of individual deep emotional factors and relationships in the causation of that behaviour. It represents the ability to see behind and beyond the more superficial and overt material causes to the real underlying personality factors, and to appreciate just as significantly the deeper emotional factors involved in one's own attitude. It is, too, the ability to work through and use these basic attitudes curatively. If I had briefly to classify the aspects in which the psychiatric approach differs from that or more orthodox case work, I think I would name these eight points:

1. The toleration of the client's antagonism, indifference or aggression without anxiety.
2. Maintenance of a therapeutic imperturbability in the face of the client's and his relatives' agitation.
3. Maintenance of an uncritical attitude towards socially unacceptable behaviour, at least until an adequate relationship has been built up.
4. Concentration on the total readjustment of the client, rather than on what is ostensibly the presenting problem or difficulty.
5. Skilled management of the relationship situation.
6. Avoidance of feelings of obligation in the client over the relief of material needs.
7. A knowledge of the mental mechanisms of the problem with its resultant ability to turn positive factors in the environment to therapeutic use and to avoid wounding the client's sensitivity even in the commonplaces of the relationship.
8. The guarding of the relationship with the client, as an absolutely confidential and individual one.

It will be seen that the use of the psychiatric approach requires not only a changed background of training and knowledge, but a special attitude on the part of the case worker also. She must be convinced of the worthwhileness and value of her work; and even when she is so convinced she will require experience and a sound basic personality if she is to tolerate the long-term slow process of psychiatric case work without the anxiety-driven urge 'to do something more objective and get quick results'. Or, for that matter, without going to the opposite extreme and losing touch with the reality situation in a welter of half-understood technical terms which seem to explain the whole world so simply to her own self, if to no one else. I am afraid that some psychiatric social workers and quite a good many psychiatrists, have not yet got beyond this 'precious' attitude themselves, so we must be doubly careful than in putting over the psychiatric approach to others we do keep a firm grip on the realities of life.

And there is yet one further group who must undetstand this basic attitude of psychiatric case work—the administrators. The teaching of social science students in the basic values and techniques of the psychiatric approach leads to one startling and rather alarming result. So many students tell you in later years of the opposition and frustration they met in practice from their seniors or their committees towards their use of this approach. Sometimes it is frankly hostile opposition—I think most of us in mental health work have encountered that at some time or other. But more often I think it is a failure to understand our purpose and our point of view—and that failure is very often our own fault as clinical workers. We are apt to regard the administrator as a non-understanding man whose main function—apart from paying our salaries—seems to be obstruction of our pet ideas. We forget that the administrator has his own side of the problem to consider, his committee to convince, his local authority treasurer to placate and his own anxiety-driven fear that he will be left holding the baby whilst we are still engrossed in the obstetric technicalities of its birth. If we do not trouble to understand his attitude or difficulties, is it so very surprising that he responds in kind and does not understand ours? That is why a conference such as this can be so valuable with its joint membership of clinicians and administrators. And doubly valuable this year because of its experimental use of the discussion group technique. Those of you with experience of group discussion work with multidisciplinary groups will know how mutual understanding, the lessening of status and inter-personal tensions and a balanced sound attitude on all sides can emerge from such a group. Remember, too, that your group experience at this conference need only be a beginning. One of the most valuable contributions we could make to mental health would be for the clinical workers and administrators in each area to get down to real group discussion of their mutual difficulties, ideas and hopes. Not only should we come to understand each other much better, but we would find in a well-run discussion group the factual and visible proof of much of what I have said about mental health today. We should see an example of the importance of working out inter-personal tensions, of understanding and accepting our feelings of aggression, over-dominance or over-dependence towards each other and of the significance of inter-personal relationships in the sense that I have described.

We in the mental health field are often accused of being too theoretical and too detached from the real situation; too fond of preaching a creed which will not work out in practice. There is at least some apparent foundation for this criticism in the condition of our own internal relationship difficulties. Of how many mental hospitals or psychiatric clinics can one honestly say that the staff morale is high or that they are free from damaging status rivalries or unworked-out inter-personal difficulties. Or for that matter, how many local health or education departments could we describe as examples of the application of sound mental health methods to the problems of staff relationships and morale? Is the sickness rate, the absentee rate, the instability of employment rate in your hospital higher than in similar neighbouring hospitals? Is your departmental staff less contented and settled and happy in their job, and therefore less efficient than other similar departments? And if so, why? If we are going to apply these principles of mental health generally to the community, we must surely first apply them to our own community units. Let us first put our own house in order before criticizing the Jones next door.

Besides which, none of our clinical case workers is going to be able to give of her best work to others if half her energies and much of her anxiety is tied up in her own difficult work situation.

Indeed, the more we examine this topic of mental health, the more we appreciate its complexity, the more we realize how closely it is linked with the everyday pattern of our lives. Is the success of your business deal related as much to the marital relationship pattern of your co-director as to the quality of your goods? How far is the hard core of chronic delinquency related to emotional deprivation of the delinquent in infancy? What are the psycho-dynamic processes at work in an international conference, and how far are the results related to special personality factors in the delegates? How far is the quality and value of leadership in a community related to the basic cultural and child-rearing patterns in that community? We have only the beginnings of answers to these problems, but they are all problems of community mental health which we must sooner or later face—and solve.

But the emphasis of this conference is—and rightly is—on the practical aspects of community mental health, on what you and I can do now. Let me then try and summarize what I conceive to be our duty in the promotion of community mental health. I do not pretend that this summary can do more than outline the picture, nor that you should accept it as it is. Rather is it an attempt to give you a starting-off point in your discussion group, where the real work of this Conference will be done and the real results obtained.

Here then are three aims which we could adopt in our work for mental health:

First the encouragement and planning and creation of a total mental health treatment service—social and psychiatric. A service to cover not only the mental hospital, the mental deficiency hospital, the psychiatric out-patient unit, the child guidance clinic, but one to treat adequately all age groups and all types of psychiatric disturbance—to deal with the socially maladjusted as well as the more overtly disturbed. To deal with those two neglected age groups, the adolescent and the aged, as well as the child and the adult. Bearing in mind always that the idea of such a community service must be to treat the patient in the community wherever possible and in hospital or institution only when other circumstances demand.

Secondly we must encourage and support adequate research into, and understanding of, the deeper motivations of human behaviour, into the mental mechanics of human relationships, into the essential importance of basic emotional factors in every sphere of human activity.

The third aim is a long-term one, but in my view none the less important for that. It is the slow, but steady spread of our developing knowledge of the root springs of human behaviour and motivation amongst all those who deal at any level with their fellow men. It is the slow building up of a mature and understanding attitude towards social problems first in ourselves and then in all those whose work involves inter-personal relationship of any kind—social worker, magistrates, administrators, legislators, employers and ultimately the whole community.

Surely it is the duty of any good social worker not only to aid her individual client, but so to direct her work that ultimately the social evil which caused that problem will cease to exist. So to modify in her own small individual way the environment so that ultimately the need for a social worker in that field will no longer exist. Perhaps you will say the emphasis is on 'ultimately' here. But if we could feel that even our own little individual help did bring that 'ultimately' a little nearer, I should be glad to think we had thereby earned the title of being good social workers in the field of community mental health.

GEORGE ALLEN & UNWIN LTD

Head office:
40 Museum Street, London, W.C.1
Telephone: 01–405 8577

Sales, Distribution and Accounts Departments
Park Lane, Hemel Hempstead, Herts.
Telephone: 0442 3244

Athens: 7 Stadiou Street, Athens 125
Auckland: P.O. Box 36013, Auckland 9
Barbados: P.O. Box 222, Bridgetown
Bombay: 103/5 Fort Street, Bombay 1
Calcutta: 285J Bepin Behari Ganguli Street, Calcutta 12
Dacca: Alico Building, 18 Motijheel, Dacca 2
Hong Kong: 105 Wing on Mansion, 26 Hankow Road, Kowloon
Ibadan: P.O. Box 62
Johannesburg: P.O. Box 23134, Joubert Park
Karachi: Karachi Chambers, McLeod Road, Karachi 2
Lahore: 22 Falletis' Hotel, Egerton Road
Madras: 2/18 Mount Road, Madras 2
Manila: P.O. Box 157, Quezon City, D-502
Mexico: Serapio Rendon 125, Mexico 4, D.F.
Nairobi: P.O. Box 30583
New Delhi: 1/18B Asaf Ali Road, New Delhi 1
Rio de Janeiro: Caixa Postal 2537–ZC–00
Singapore: 36c Prinsep Street, Singapore 7
Sydney N.S.W. 2000: Bradbury House, 55 York Street
Tokyo: C.P.O. Box 1728, Tokyo 100/91
Toronto: 145 Adelaide Street West, Toronto 1

The Development of Personality

T. A. RATCLIFFE

From the background of his own clinical experience, Dr Ratcliffe as a child Psychiatrist and his considerable and wide experience in the training of these professional workers, has concentrated on the integration of theory with practice. It is not written as a theoretical 'text-book'; it is intended to stimulate further technical reading by its emphasis on the practical application in 'real-life' situations of basic theoretical learning.

Although this book was written primarily for the professional worker and the professional student in this field, it could be read with value and interest by others such as magistrates, marriage guidance counsellors and youth leaders, and last, but by no means least, by parents.

'A well-written and sensible approach to what is becoming a complex and mystifying subject for the layman. I would highly recommend it to both layman and new mother . . . skilfully and readably organised.' *British Hospital Journal*

Treatment for Children

THE WORK OF A CHILD GUIDANCE CLINIC

D. T. MACLAY

Although many books dealing with the Treatment of Children have been written by analysts, few psychologists and psychiatrists who treat children are analytically trained. For this reason a book written by a non-analyst with wide experience of therapy will be particularly welcome to psychiatrists, psychologists, social workers and child guidance clinics, paediatricians, school medical or welfare officers and general practitioners who are regularly confronted with children's problems, but who have no analytical training. It should also be of interest to parents, teachers, social workers and play leaders who are not especially concerned with problems of children but who wish to deepen their understanding of child behaviour.

LONDON · GEORGE ALLEN AND UNWIN LTD